THE BETTER WAY TO DRINK

MODERATION & CONTROL OF PROBLEM DRINKING

ROGER E. VOGLER, PH.D.
WAYNE R. BARTZ, PH.D.

This paperback edition published 1985
by New Harbinger Publications, Inc.
2200 Adeline, Suite 305
Oakland, CA 94607

(Original hardcover edition published 1982
by Simon & Schuster, a Division of Gulf & Western Corporation)

ISBN 0-934986-16-9 (paperback)
ISBN 0-671-44944-3 (hardcover)

To our parents,
Dee and Herb, Audrey and Art,
who rose above their world of limited opportunities
and encouraged our pursuit of knowledge and
personal growth in so many ways

Acknowledgments

WE ARE GRATEFUL to the following people who read a draft of the book and gave us many helpful suggestions for improvement: Jim Donnelly, Jane Gray, Bill Haney, Linda Hamel, Bud Martin, Marianne Rasor, Terry Sandbek, John Taylor, John Uphold, Holly Webber, and Gary Wild. The editorial expertise of Gerald Martin, Dick Rasor, and Hedy and Lionel White were particularly valuable to us in refining the quality of the book. Roger Benton and Nancy Webber were completing their doctoral research on tolerance in our laboratory at the time we were writing the book. We thank Roger for his careful examination of many aspects of the technical and scientific material in the book. Nancy's review from a clinical as well as technical perspective was also especially helpful. Ted Weissbach and John Compton played important roles in much of our earlier research and deserve a special word of acknowledgment, as does Bill Banks for his contributions to our more recent research on tolerance. We thank Ted Hopson for his professional assistance and are grateful for the hard work of our typists Jo Brueckner and Carolyn Larsen. Finally, we appreciate the helpful input from our editors at Simon and Schuster, Fred Hills and Bob Bender.

Contents

Introduction

THIS BOOK WAS written to help two groups of people: those who wish to make changes in their use of alcohol, and those who are concerned about someone else's drinking. Successful drinkers are given guidelines on how to stay that way and prevent future trouble; problem drinkers are provided with specific, practical methods to reduce their consumption to moderate levels; and serious alcohol abusers are told how to quit drinking entirely and enjoy life sober. Concerned relatives and friends will find suggestions on how, where, and when they can help the drinker as well as when they cannot help.

Nearly everybody knows someone who drinks too much. Many excessive drinkers are themselves aware that they abuse alcohol, but do not know how to change. Often they are afraid to discuss their drinking with anyone because they have typically been told to quit or cut down by using willpower, which they have tried without success. We will *not* tell drinkers that alcohol is sinful, that they *must* quit (unless they are serious abusers), or that they have to declare themselves to be weak, miserable, or pathetic "alcoholics" before they can do better. We *will* tell drinkers, their families and friends, something they already know: that drinking is an acceptable and enjoyable part of life if kept under control. Only when control is lost does drinking lead to physical, social, and personal disaster.

Fortunately, it *is* possible to maintain drinking within safe and moderate limits by closely monitoring blood alcohol, controlling consumption, and drinking sanely and successfully. Abstinence is not the only solution to unsuccessful drinking. *The majority of problem drinkers can learn moderation,* but until now there has been no help for them! This book is based on our fifteen years of research to develop new and more effective methods of changing drinking habits. (The scientific basis for this approach is reviewed in the Appendix.) These techniques have been used extensively with drinkers of all types in our clinical practice. Until now, these methods have not been available to the public. They are practical and they work. Use them and you and your loved ones *can* drink successfully!

PART I Why the Successful Drinking Approach Works

CHANGE IN DRINKING habits is possible because, contrary to what you have been told, the excessive use of alcohol is *not* a "disease." Drinking is a learned behavior and excessive drinkers have simply developed a habit of overdrinking in the same way that overeaters or heavy smokers have learned their excessive habits. Given the strong social encouragement to drink, without any guidelines for successful drinking, many people, not surprisingly, abuse alcohol. Friends, relatives, TV, films, and advertising often encourage us to drink too much. The specific kinds of drinking habits people acquire depend on cultural, family, and peer influences. Social skills for meeting needs, alternative satisfactions, and tolerance to the effects from prior drinking also affect the amount one drinks. Drinking has an impact not only on our body but on our job, marriage, children, social relationships, and self-image. We are legally responsible for knowing our blood alcohol level when we drive, yet few people clearly understand the relationship between consumption and blood alcohol. Such training is simply not available. We will provide that information, explore the pros and cons of drinking, and clarify the differences between the successful and unsuccessful uses of alcohol.

11

1

Drinking: A Habit,
Not a Disease

Excessive drinking is a learned pattern of behavior. Yet one of the catchphrases of our time is "alcoholism is a disease." Many "authorities" insist that alcohol abuse is literally an illness that a person either has or does not have. We are all familiar with the term "alcoholic," but you may be surprised to hear that there is no commonly accepted definition. *The Dictionary of Words About Alcohol* has ten pages of definitions of "alcoholism" and "alcoholic." Most alcohol counselors support the disease approach, yet unlike other diseases alcoholism cannot be "caught" through biological means; there is no alcoholism virus, fungus, or germ. Alcoholism is not borne through the air like the cold virus; you cannot sneeze and give someone alcoholism. It is not carried by parasites the way malaria and yellow fever are; no flea or mosquito can bite you and give you alcoholism. You cannot get alcoholism accidentally as you can a broken leg, and you are not born with it as some would claim. If alcoholism were actually a disease, it would be the only disease that is sold conveniently packaged, that produces a huge revenue for the government, that is habit-forming and results in arrests, fines, and even jail sentences. It would be the only disease that is a contributing cause in over half the highway deaths in this country, provokes crime, and is spread by advertising. According to Mark Keller, editor of the *Journal of Studies on Alcohol* and a supporter of the disease

13

definition, it is a disease "of unknown etiology [cause] and unknown site." If we look at the question realistically, we must see that the excessive use of alcohol can and does result in physical disease, and sometimes physical addiction. But drinking itself, including heavy drinking, is not caused by disease but by learning. You must *voluntarily* consume alcohol in fairly large amounts before you have an alcohol problem.

Why then do some insist upon calling the overuse of alcohol a disease? There are good social reasons for doing so. Over the past century, more and more undesirable behaviors have been redefined by authorities as "sickness" rather than as moral violations or crimes. Murderers, shoplifters, child molesters, or even bored housewives are said to be "sick," victims of "mental illness," and are not held fully responsible for their behavior. While Alcoholics Anonymous has fostered the explanation of a physical difference as the cause of the "disease of alcoholism," medicine, and psychiatry in particular, has unfortunately added the dimension "mental disorder." Alcohol abuse is a relative newcomer to this movement to consider problems in living as mental illness. Only in recent years have the American Medical Association (1968), the National Institute on Alcohol Abuse and Alcoholism (1974), and the World Health Organization (1957) mounted an effort to redefine alcohol abuse as a form of illness. One obvious motive is to decriminalize alcoholic behavior and thereby make it more likely that abusers will seek help on their own. Instead of suffering legal consequences for abusive drinking, the alcoholic may be considered the victim of an illness and therefore treated with kindness and concern. A problem drinker is thereby relieved of the responsibility for uncontrolled drinking, just as most patients are not blamed for their illnesses. However, this change in thinking has simply substituted the negative concept of sickness or mental illness for the negative notions of moral weakness or criminality. In our opinion, the trade-off has not succeeded in encouraging people with a drinking problem to voluntarily do something about it.

An additional offshoot of labeling excessive drinking a disease is that alcoholism was brought under the wings of the medical establishment. Only then could Congress legitimately provide funds for a

National Institute on Alcohol Abuse and Alcoholism to treat, find cures for, or prevent the "disease." Note that it is unlikely that Congress would or could have funded a National Institute on Bad Habits (which might include smoking, overeating, swearing, excessive drinking, and gambling). Society feels sorry for and wants to help people with a disease, but those with bad habits are expected to take care of their own problems!

Why should alcohol abuse alone be called a disease while other abusive behaviors such as smoking and overeating are considered bad habits? All are harmful physically. All are economic liabilities and can generate degrees of personal and social difficulty. Physical ailments can indeed be a consequence but are not a cause of any of these behaviors. It is clear that we must look to *social* factors in order to understand why alcohol abuse is the only one of these destructive behaviors generally claimed to be a disease.

Smoking, overeating, and excessive drinking all result from a complex cluster of influences: cultural rules, parental and peer influences, easy availability of the abused substance, desire for a change in mood or feelings, ignorance, inadequacy of social skills, lack of satisfying alternatives, and perhaps to a minor degree some biological predisposition. The two main reasons for giving alcohol abuse special status are: (1) the greater problems caused for others by drinking, and (2) the enthusiastic promotion of the "disease" approach by Alcoholics Anonymous.

When people overeat or smoke they may influence their own health, but they rarely directly affect others (although we are now concerned about possible hazards in "secondhand" smoke). People who drink too much clearly *do* affect others. They sometimes kill or maim with drunk driving, may go into a rage and attack a loved one, lose their jobs, destroy their families, or abuse their children. Drinking may indeed affect the drinker's entire life pattern and *everybody in it*. Smokers and overeaters rarely have such major direct impact upon the lives of others. They can be ignored, but heavy drinkers often force us to react. Recognizing this, Alcoholics Anonymous has for many years tried to make treatment for alcohol problems more readily available and acceptable. And for *serious* abusers, or alcoholics, AA has probably been the single most valuable source of help. In our opinion, however, fostering the stereotype of the alcohol abuser as a helpless, out-of-control victim of a terrible disease has actually made it *more* difficult for many excessive drinkers to acknowledge their problem until the situation becomes desperate. Generally, the result is that only the most extreme abusers are identified and offered treatment. Nobody wants to admit being "sick," especially mentally, unless the problem is serious. (Imagine a situation where you could not be called overweight or do anything about reducing until you were a hundred pounds above normal, admitted you were "sick," and then the only cure offered was to stop eating—completely!)

Our approach to excessive drinking provides a positive alternative to the historic mistreatment of drinkers as criminals and to the disease approach. We view excessive alcohol consumption as a learned behavior pattern or habit, just like overeating, smoking, or swearing. Habits, whether labeled good or bad, occur in varying degrees and are determined by an individual's entire life experience along with a variety of continuing social and physical consequences. Viewed from this social learning approach, the drinker is not faced with a choice of being or not being an alcoholic; rather, drinking can be measured along a continuous scale from no drinking at all at one extreme to excessive and harmful drinking at the other. If a person's drinking becomes excessive, a host of negative consequences may begin to occur—such as physical ailments, vocational problems, social and marital discord, and legal and economic troubles. These unhappy consequences may themselves increase consumption and thus the problem is compounded.

In contrast, when drinking and its consequences are called an illness, the undesirable label "alcoholic" comes into play and the drinker is often discouraged by the label itself from seeking help. Since smokers and overeaters rarely interfere much with others' happiness, they are not subject to such negative labels and are more willing to seek help. Just look around at the popularity of private clinics and organizations for smokers and overeaters, such as the Schick centers and Weight Watchers, plus the great popularity of fad diets and smoking cures. In contrast, help for the mild alcohol abuser at an early stage (when drinking habits are most easily changed) is usually not available. Even if it were, most would probably avoid being labeled an alcoholic and would therefore not seek out such help. We have all seen the reactions of friends and relatives when someone announces enrollment in a weight-loss class or program. "Great!" "Wonderful!" "More power to you!" But what would be the reactions to an announcement like "You'll never guess what course I'm taking at the community college. It's a class on how to drink moderately." The listener might indeed say "Great!" but later would find much to gossip about. "Wait until you hear what Fred told me tonight. He's taking a course in controlling his drinking. He must have a problem with booze. Do you suppose he's an alcoholic?"

Dr. Morris Chafetz, first director of the National Institute on Alcohol Abuse and Alcoholism, writes: "The fundamental problem we face is not the use of alcohol. . . . That is a fact of the human condition we cannot change. The problem is misuse, irresponsible use, of the substance." It is interesting to note that other important members of professions that have traditionally supported the disease approach have begun to acknowledge the learned nature of drinking habits. Dr. Alfred Smith, a psychiatrist who spent fifteen years seeking a biological cause for alcoholism, remarked before the National Safety Congress in Chicago, "It's a terrible disappointment to me to finally face up to the fact that alcoholism is a behavior disorder."

The simple reality is that most Americans drink, and the great majority drink sensibly. Those who do not drink sensibly are usually afraid to admit it to others or to themselves because of social costs such as possible job loss, rejection by friends and relatives, and reduction in self-esteem. Possibly the most important unfortunate consequence is being treated as a victim of "the disease of alcoholism," with total abstinence offered as the only cure.

With a few exceptions (such as those who have been seriously harmed physically or socially by drinking), a far more realistic and effective approach would be to learn controlled, moderate drinking habits under conditions which increase self-respect and dignity rather than degrade the individual. According to this approach, the drinker is regarded not as a passive victim of a disease process but as an intelligent, responsible person capable of making and carrying out decisions about his or her own welfare.

Our primary purpose in writing this book is to make it as easy for people who drink excessively to receive and comfortably accept help in changing their habits as it is for overeaters or smokers to get help. Our approach stresses early self-identification of "drinking too much" and responsible action by the drinker in the direction of moderate, controlled drinking habits.

Let's take a look at an example of someone who drinks too much and could improve the situation if only he knew what to do.

THE CASE OF MARK

Mark is a thirty-eight-year-old successful businessman who has been concerned about his drinking for a number of years. No one except his wife suspects him of having a problem, and she is not seriously worried. By most standards, Mark is a success in everything he does. His marriage is reasonably stable, his children love him, and he loves them. His parents, in-laws, and friends all enjoy Mark as a socially skillful and pleasant person. His associates at work regard him as an intelligent and conscientious colleague whose competence is unquestioned. So, Mark is not noteworthy in any negative sense and certainly no one regards him as an alcoholic. Only Mark himself really knows how much he drinks and only he worries about it from time to time. Mark is aware that he is consuming more alcohol now than a few years ago and it bothers him that he looks forward so much to becoming somewhat "high" every evening. He notices that he doesn't have the kind of control over his drinking that he has over practically everything else in his life. He has checked around for sources of help and has come up with three possibilities: Alcoholics Anonymous, his family doctor, or psychological counseling. But Mark does not regard himself as an alcoholic and he is not religiously inclined, so what he knows about Alcoholics Anonymous and its religious philosophy pretty well rules him out as a potential member.

Besides, he does not want to stop drinking altogether. Mark knows that his family doctor would probably just tell him to cut down or stop drinking, and might prescribe a tranquilizer. Counseling doesn't really appeal to him, since he does not believe he has any major personal problems or needs his "head shrunk."

Our work with alcohol abusers suggests that Mark can successfully learn to drink moderately. There are several reasons why. He has never been treated for an alcohol problem and has not lost work because of drinking. He has on occasion gone to work with a hangover, but persevered and managed to perform adequately. His physical health is generally good and his family seems to be flourishing. Mark knows he is drinking too much and is aware that drinking accompanies almost all of his nonwork activities and social engagements. Also, Mark is aware and concerned about the fact that he selects his friends partly because they too enjoy drinking, many of them to excess.

Mark estimates that he drinks about 6 ounces of Scotch each weekday and between 8 and 12 ounces per day on weekends. However, if he actually took the trouble to record his consumption for a couple of weeks, he would find his average weekday consumption to be 8 ounces of 80-proof Scotch and his average weekend consumption to be well over 12 ounces per day. (He would also find that writing down each drink might actually reduce his consumption somewhat by making him more aware of the amount and frequency of intake and perhaps a little self-conscious about it. This, as you will soon see, is partly why we recommend that people record how much they drink.)

Mark needs to take a close look at the *situations* in which he drinks. A typical weekday for Mark goes something like this: He usually returns home from work about 5:00 P.M. The first thing he does when he walks in the door is pour himself a tumbler full of Scotch on the rocks without measuring. Usually he carries his drink around the house while he changes his clothes, reads the newspaper, watches the TV news, and involves himself in other passive activities until dinner time. Mark is aware of his tendency to put off dinner in order to prolong his drinking period. Over the past several years it has become routine for the children to eat at 6:00 P.M. so he and his wife could drink until 7:30 or 8:00 P.M. when they eat dinner.

Incidentally, Mark is aware that his wife's consumption has also increased significantly over the past several years. He feels somewhat guilty about his influence on her drinking since he encourages her to do so, mixes her drinks, and secretly worries about her potential for abuse as well as his. During the lengthy cocktail hour before dinner, Mark drinks until he feels quite high. Since he weighs 160 pounds and consumes around 8 ounces of Scotch during this time, the amount of alcohol in his blood by dinner time is considerable. However, after dinner Mark rarely continues drinking and does not feel so high because food slows down the absorption of alcohol into the bloodstream. So, unless he plans to get really loaded, which he might do on a Friday or Saturday, he usually stops drinking after dinner.

Very little family interaction takes place in Mark's household. The children are usually in bed by 9:30, his wife tending the children so that Mark can indulge himself in his usual passive activities. Typically, he sits before the television set until about 10:00 P.M. His wife often has to awaken him to tell him it is time for bed because he has dozed off. His sleepiness is largely due to the alcohol he has consumed. On those occasional evenings when Mark drinks very little he can stay up until midnight and feel quite alert and active. When he does retire, Mark does not sleep soundly or wake up the next morning feeling refreshed and full of energy. His eight to nine hours in bed each night are restless and often interrupted by the need to use the bathroom. Also, his drinking interferes with his ability to perform sexually, and therefore he and his wife have sex only occasionally. Mark is unhappy about this change since they once had an active and highly satisfying love life. But that was before he drank so much.

In the morning, Mark often takes aspirin to relieve his headache and general "blahs." Since he does not want his wife to know he is suffering from a hangover, which might arouse her concern about his drinking too much, Mark usually takes the aspirin in secret. Because of his relative youth and generally good health, he is usually able to throw off any remaining effects of hangover by midmorning. While Mark often feels sluggish and tired when he first gets to work, he typically drinks several cups of coffee to get going. Moreover, he is a good worker and disciplines himself rather well to be productive. Mark's associates at work know him to be a fair but occasionally irritable person. Mark is aware that his episodes of irritability are usually related to the aftereffects of drinking, but he never says anything to anyone about it.

While Mark knows that his drinking has been increasing over several years, he regards it as having become a clear problem only about two years ago. He and his wife at that time were in conflict over family economics and did not seem to be communicating well. A series of major arguments occurred while he was trying to expand his role at work and was suffering the pressure of additional responsibilities and job-related problems. As a consequence of these stresses, Mark began to drink more, rarely going a day without alcohol. One evening he had a great deal to drink and ended up in a long confrontation with his wife. The Scotch ran out, so he got in his car and drove to the liquor store to buy another bottle. Because of his anger and his intoxication, he ended up being stopped by the police for fast and reckless driving. When they discovered that he had been drinking, they put him through their quick check for intoxication, the Field Sobriety Test, which he failed. He then was handcuffed and taken to the police station, given a breath test to determine his blood alcohol, booked for drunk driving, and confined to a cell overnight.

The next day he consulted an attorney, who advised him that since his blood alcohol reading was well beyond the legal intoxication level, it would be very difficult to have the drunk driving charge reduced to reckless driving. Mark ultimately suffered the social embarrassment of a court experience, expensive attorney's fees, a heavy fine from the court, an increase in his car insurance premiums, not to mention the mortification of spending the night in jail and the painful disclosure of the episode to his wife and a few intimates. You might think that all this would have cured Mark's drinking problem; he did cut down temporarily, but before long his alcohol intake gradually increased to the same level as before.

Mark is under no particular pressure from his associates or his wife to change his drinking habits (other than an occasional comment from his wife about drinking a bit less). Privately, Mark is concerned that his drinking is a serious problem and is aware that by himself he cannot seem to change it. He does not want to stop drinking entirely. Nor does he consider himself an alcoholic at this point. His understanding of the Alcoholics Anonymous program suggests that he cannot accept their approach. The open and public admission of being an alcoholic, recognizing abstinence as the only cure, and accepting their religious philosophy are particularly against his beliefs. Mark also knows that he is not "sick." He does not have a disease. In short, from Mark's point of view, no acceptable means of help is available other than so-called willpower, which hasn't worked.

We maintain there *are* steps Mark can take to change his drinking habits without considering himself an alcoholic or seeking professional help. We will return to Mark later, but first it is essential that we understand some important information about alcohol, recognize the effects of social influence on drinking, and explore the basics of self-control.

2

It's a Wet World

A three-thousand-year-old inscription on the wall of an Egyptian tomb reads:

> If I kiss her and her lips are open,
> I am happy even without beer.

Alcoholic beverages are as old as human culture itself. Virtually every society, from that of the stone age to modern technological, has known how to produce some variety of intoxicating liquor. This is not surprising, of course, since efforts to preserve most fruit juices will inevitably lead to experience with fermentation and the natural production of alcohol—interesting things happen to stored juice!

Also, as was noted by our Egyptian wall-scribbler, humans readily observe that alcohol (as well as a kiss) has natural enjoyable properties—its pleasant effects are shared common knowledge across time and cultures. *How* alcohol is actually used in a culture is a matter determined by each age and society. Some societies attempt to prohibit the use of alcohol altogether (the Moslem countries are today's most noteworthy example). Some societies have considered alcohol to be a gift from the gods—the ancient Romans honored Bacchus, the god of wine, and sometimes considered drunkenness to be a form of worship. Alcohol has been used by governments as a method of social control, as in Great Britain during the industrial revolution when "penny gin" was made available to help keep the "lower classes" quiet (that penny gin was a glassful and probably kept a lot of folks at least drunk if not quiet).

Alcohol has been viewed in most cultures as a mixed blessing—a source of pleasure, relaxation, and social stimulation as well as sometimes a source of destructive physical addiction and a contributor to personal, social, and financial disaster.

Each of us as an individual drinks (or abstains) in large part as a result of pure chance, determined by the culture and family into which we happen to have been born. Each society has its own specific rules for drinking, and these rules are clearly related to the frequency of abuse when countries are compared. Cultural drinking rules are agreed-upon ways of consumption in various situations and on various occasions. For example, in the Italian culture, it is customary to drink wine in moderate amounts with meals, but not usually at other times. Becoming intoxicated is frowned upon, and Italian women will not go out with men who have had too much to drink. Contrast this with the Irish culture, in which it is customary (for men anyway) to consume large amounts of hard liquor at almost any time with the clear purpose of becoming intoxicated. This difference in cultural rules for drinking is tied to the relatively lower incidence of alcohol abuse among Italians as compared to the Irish, even though Italian consumption is quite high.

While working some years ago with alcohol abusers in Germany, we were astounded to discover that the mental hospital treating alcoholics (as well as other mental patients) served strong beer in the snack bar. They explained, "Why, beer isn't alcohol, it's *beer*, the staff of life—like bread, meat, or potatoes. How could a person be expected to do without beer?" Impossible to imagine—at least in Bavaria, where they deliver beer daily to your doorstep and pick up a rack of empties (much as milkmen once did throughout America). Even McDonald's hamburger restaurants in Germany serve draft beer. In fact, we've never been in a family restaurant in Germany that didn't serve beer.

The Germans dearly love their beer, and the American culture is also very "wet" despite occasional attempts to dry it out. As history makes clear, the Prohibition experiment of the 1920s and 1930s was a complete failure and, if anything, may have made drinking problems in America even worse. If we are going to deal effectively with the hazards of alcohol in modern life, it is necessary and realistic to simply acknowledge its presence and ready availability, now and for the foreseeable future.

Recent figures indicate that among major countries of the world the United States ranks fifteenth in annual consumption with about 2.1 gallons of pure (100 percent or 200-proof) alcohol per person (equivalent to about 5.3 gallons of 80-proof liquor). In terms of ethanol volume, Poland leads the world in consumption of distilled spirits and Portugal in the consumption of wine. The West Germans put away the greatest quantity of beer, but the Australians drink stronger beer and therefore actually consume more ethanol.

As you can see, despite the basic physical similarities between the peoples of different cultural background, total alcohol consumed and choice of beverage vary widely. This emphasizes the powerful effect that society has on drinking behavior.

While we all grow up under the influence of cultural drinking rules, we also are raised in a unique *family* setting. It has been said that the decision to drink is made by our parents, not by us. Parental drinking patterns strongly influence the later drinking done by children. We should point out that it is not what parents *say* about drinking that counts, but rather, *how they drink*. If the parents are seen by their children to engage in heavy drinking, it is likely that the children will imitate their parents and also learn to drink heavily.

During teenage years, as youngsters move further away from family bonds and parental models, the behavior of friends becomes a growing influence in molding beginning drinking habits. The latest available data suggest that about 75 percent of high school students will begin to drink during those four years. Teenagers' friends can eventually have more day-to-day influence than parents. Because drinking is encouraged in many ways in our society, there is a great deal of social pressure for teens to drink. Young people often believe that drinking, like smoking, automatically bestows grown-up status (which they typically seek). The assumed connection between adulthood and drinking is strengthened by advertising, which depicts at-

APPARENT PER CAPITA CONSUMPTION,[1] IN GALLONS, OF ALCOHOLIC BEVERAGES BY PERSONS 15 YEARS OLD AND OLDER IN 26 COUNTRIES[2]

Rank	Country	Year of Latest Data	Distilled Spirits		Wine		Beer		Total	
			Beverage Volume	Ethanol Volume	Beverage Volume	Ethanol Volume	Beverage Volume	Ethanol Volume	Persons 15 Yrs. and Older	Entire Population
1.	Portugal	1974	1.20[3]	0.46	43.91	5.27	10.87	0.54	6.27	4.60
2.	France	1972	2.34	0.80	37.40	4.07	20.11[6]	0.99	5.87	4.43
3.	Italy	1973	1.32	0.66	37.91	3.79	4.74	0.24	4.69	3.55
4.	Switzerland	1971–73	1.88	0.75	15.41	1.70	28.72[3,6]	1.39	3.85	2.95
5.	Spain	1971	2.67	1.07	19.83	2.18	1.34	0.53	3.78	2.85
6.	W. Germany	1974	2.39[3]	0.91	7.78	0.82	50.50	2.02	3.75	2.88
7.	Austria	1972	2.10	0.84	11.87	1.25	36.30	1.63	3.72	2.79
8.	Belgium	1973	1.21	0.61	5.26	0.63	48.90[6]	2.15	3.39	2.61
9.	Australia	1972–73	0.82[3]	0.47	3.71	0.45	48.08	2.40	3.32	2.36
10.	Hungary	1972	2.00[3]	1.00	13.36	1.54	19.70	0.69	3.23	2.51
11.	New Zealand	1972	0.85[3]	0.49	2.94	0.35	46.85	2.34	3.18	2.17
12.	Czechoslovakia	1973	2.29	0.92	4.66	0.57	49.69	1.49	2.98	2.30
13.	Canada	1974	2.54[3]	1.01	2.00	0.32	30.27	1.51	2.84	2.07
14.	Denmark	1973	1.25	0.53	3.69	0.55	38.85	1.71	2.79	2.14
15.	U.S.A.[2]	1976	2.65	1.14	2.34	0.34	29.03	1.31	2.78	2.08
16.	United Kingdom	1974	0.93[3]	0.53	2.32	0.28	38.92	1.94	2.76	2.11
17.	Netherlands	1974	1.94[3]	0.97	3.66	0.44	26.74	1.34	2.75	2.04

18.	Ireland[2]	1975	1.36[3]	0.78	1.31	0.14	32.43	1.56	2.47	1.70
19.	Soviet Union[7]	1972	3.30[3]	1.22	6.05[3]	0.91	6.93[3]	0.21	2.34[7]	1.69
20.	Poland	1974	2.87	1.43	2.40	0.29	12.94	0.49	2.21	1.63
21.	Finland[2]	1976	2.81	1.07	1.60	0.24	17.58	0.82	2.14	1.61
22.	Sweden	1973	2.23	0.87	2.42	0.30	15.17	0.67	1.84	1.46
23.	Japan[2]	1974	1.33[3,4]	0.44	5.60[3,5]	0.86	11.63	0.46	1.77	1.34
24.	Norway	1974	1.47	0.63	1.11	0.15	15.24	0.69	1.47	1.11
25.	Iceland	1973	2.30	0.94	0.85	0.10	6.01	0.12	1.16	0.76
26.	Israel	1974	0.97	0.48	1.47	0.18	3.96	0.20	0.86	0.58

SOURCE: Data updated from Mark Keller and Carol Gurioli, *Statistics on Consumption of Alcohol and on Alcoholism.* New Brunswick, N.J.: Rutgers Center of Alcohol Studies, 1976.

NOTE: Only per capita consumption by actual drinkers produces a satisfactory comparison among countries. For the same years as shown in the table, consumption of ethanol per drinker has been calculated for the following countries: Canada, 3.56 gallons; U.S., 3.92 gallons; Ireland, 4.35 gallons; Finland, 3.38 gallons.

[1] For comparative purposes only.

[2] A drinking age population other than 15 years and older seems more accurate in at least these countries: U.S, 14 years and older, total consumption in this group—2.69 gallons; Ireland, 18 years and older, total consumption in this group—2.68 gallons; and Japan, 20 years and older, total consumption in this group—1.90 gallons.

[3] Values converted from ethanol.

[4] Includes shochu.

[5] Includes saki.

[6] Includes cider.

[7] Illegally produced samogon is estimated to increase total consumption to about 2.97 gallons per capita.

Reprinted from the *Third Special Report to the U.S. Congress on Alcohol and Health,* Secretary of Health, Education, and Welfare, June 1978.

tractive young adults in "fun situations" such as at a beach, a concert, or on a mountain trail, laughing and having a great time while drinking. (Such ads never show young people after too many drinks, vomiting, belligerent, and ugly.)

Special subcultural influences such as gangs, clubs, or the military sometimes encourage heavy drinking by young people. For example, military bases often make alcohol available at low cost and encourage starting early in the day by selling drinks at reduced prices prior to the evening hours. Coming back sober from a three-day pass might indicate that a leave was no fun. Being able to "hold your liquor" (and that means a *lot* of liquor) is often a source of pride among military personnel.

Anthony Herbert, in his book *Soldier*, graphically describes the paratrooper tradition of "prop-blast parties." This initiation rite for new people requires the "blaster" to first consume an entire fifth of liquor (he gets his choice of bourbon, gin, rum, or Scotch) while doing pushups. He then dons a rubber raincoat (to increase body heat) and sets off on a five-mile trot. Halfway along, each blaster is met with a water glass full of his chosen booze, downs that, and continues on, if possible, to the finish at the officers' club. There he must jump from the second story into a vat of mud, then climb out for the traditional steel helmet full of vodka and champagne. Once that is empty, the "final trick" is to make it to the desk by the door of the club and sign in on the log. After one such party in which he was a blaster, Herbert notes that they had to carry one of their friends to the post hospital "since he seemed to have stopped breathing." While most military functions may not equal these prop-blast parties, almost all socializing on military bases includes drinking, and usually heavy drinking at that. The nondrinker can feel virtually left out.

The point here is not to condemn the military, but to make it clear that alcohol is very much a part of contemporary life. Recent estimates indicate that more than 70 percent of Americans aged fifteen and older drink, and this percentage has grown steadily since the days of Prohibition. The biggest increase in drinking has occurred among women. While establishing their right to full equality, they also have tended to adopt heavier drinking patterns more similar to those of men. For both sexes, then, drinking usually begins in adolescence and reaches its peak between the midtwenties and early forties. Of course, these are just averages, and your own drinking history may be different.

What about the economics of alcohol? Americans spend more than $20 *billion* each year on alcoholic beverages, and a large share of that money goes to federal, state, and local authorities in the form of excise and sales taxes. It is ironic that a custom that creates so many problems is a major source of support for the government. In fact, as a source of federal income, tax revenues from the sale of alcoholic beverages are so large that they are exceeded *only* by personal and corporate income taxes!

The average drinking-age American's alcohol consumption of 2.1 gallons a year translates into 21 quarts of 80-proof liquor or some 23 cases of beer. From studies of drinking patterns, however, it appears that 50 percent of the alcohol is consumed by about 10 percent of the drinkers. In other words, the large majority of drinkers consume less than 2.1 gallons, while a small proportion drink considerably more. While most adult Americans drink, we should keep in mind that the vast majority drink sensibly. Only about 5 percent to 7 percent of drinkers are what could be called "severe alcohol abusers." A larger number drink "excessively" but without serious life-consequences. In response to the growing concern about alcohol problems in American society, the National Institute on Alcohol Abuse and Alcoholism was formed in 1970 (the Hughes Act), giving increasing recognition to the fact that alcohol abuse is the number-one drug problem in the United States today. Unlike other substances that are frequently abused, alcohol alone is commercially available without prescription. Moreover, various cultural rules foster the development of early drinking habits. Liquor ads often portray drinkers as smooth and sophisticated. The implication is that one who is successful drinks.

The social encouragement in advertising to drink *excessively* can be strong indeed. For example, a recent beer commercial states that "some drinks are made to sip, but (our beer) is best enjoyed when you drink heartily." (We then observe the level in a glass falling rapidly between large gulps.) Schlitz ads have told us for years to "go for the gusto," suggesting that we have to cut loose and enjoy—presumably while downing lots of Schlitz. Meanwhile our young people are given contradictory messages *not* to drink and are given no guidelines about how to drink sensibly. Alcohol education, like sex education, is not taught in schools and rarely in the home, but rather in the streets. Most people begin to drink through trial-and-error experience. The choice of whether or not to drink is influenced more by social and commercial pressures than by any considered rational analysis of the question.

We know that television is a potent source of influence for young people. Consider the example of the popular "TV drunk," portrayed by the comical Foster Brooks or Dean Martin, laughing it up with a snootful while the audience howls in approval.

Cute bar napkins often promote the "fun" approach to drunkenness. One example, produced by the Fort Howard Paper Company, shows drinkers after each highball becoming ever more out of control. Headlined "Have Another," the cartoon characters are shown carrying out various "tests" to see if they have reached their limit. At each drinking level, it becomes obvious that another drink is warranted regardless of the condition of the drinker. For example, after one drink the drinker is asked to close his eyes and attempt to touch the bar. If he is successful, he can order a second drink. By the third drink he must be able to smile and think of his wife at the same time. By the seventh drink he is required to put change in his pocket without missing (three tries are allowed). The cartoon characters, after a few drinks, are shown in various states of disorientation—staggering, red-nosed, coat inside out, slopping drinks in their own faces. By the ninth drink the drinker is expected to be capable of leaving the bar under his own power and with a dignified expression. The cartoon shows a sodden drunk crawling out on all fours.

In addition to the funny drunk, another common character of film and TV is the Macho Man. Hard drinking is likely to be part of his style and credentials for heroism. While Macho Man rapidly puts away great amounts of liquor, maybe even for breakfast, it typically does not bother him (although others drop like flies). Just part of being a "real man." Sometimes the media drinker is portrayed as the pathetic out-of-control drunk, compulsively driven to gulp one drink after another. Alcohol eventually destroys his job, family relations, and life in general. The woman drinker is usually shown as a frazzled housewife, with booze as her only escape from the endless toil of cooking and cleaning, monster kids, and a brutish and unsympathetic husband. How often have you heard a TV or film character say "I need a drink." He or she then typically takes a big jolt in response to some problem situation, modeling drinking as a way to escape from stress rather than as a normal part of socializing with friends or of pleasant recreation. Television and movies are unlikely to help people learn to drink successfully. Moderate and controlled consumption, either as a positive part of the daily routine (like the cocktail hour) or as an occasional part of a mature person's social behavior, is not commonly presented, especially in programs that children or adolescents are likely to watch.

The bottom line in all this is that the media's advertising and portrayal of the hard-drinking hero, funny drunk, or disintegrating alcoholic all give the viewer no clue as to how one might appropriately use alcohol. Viewers are systematically taught to abuse, not use. This training reaps a bitter harvest. In our opinion, it is not at all surprising that many people in our society develop maladaptive drinking habits. It is indeed a wet world.

In the next chapter we will discuss the effects of alcohol on the body and behavior. This will help you decide how much alcohol you can enjoy without any harm to yourself or to others.

3

Booze and the Body

What happens when you drink? Drink enough, of course, and you get drunk. Your body has to handle in some manner anything you send down your throat. How alcohol is processed is important because each of us has a great deal of control over how quickly the level of alcohol in our blood increases and how high it finally goes. Blood Alcohol, or BA, is commonly used to measure one's level of intoxication. It refers to the percentage of alcohol in the blood. A BA reading of .10 means that one-tenth of a percent of the blood is alcohol or, in other words, there is one part alcohol in 1,000 parts of blood. (Incidentally, over thirty-five states regard this reading of .10 as the minimum BA for the presumption of "driving under the influence.")

A convenient way to understand the safety of varying degrees of intoxication is to get rid of the awkward decimal and think of blood alcohol as if it were miles-per-hour (as we will do throughout the rest of the book). Fifty-five miles per hour is the legal highway speed limit in the United States. A blood alcohol of .055 can be thought of as similar to 55 mph (just move the decimal three places to the right). Consider 55 *to be the limit with a car or a bottle.* If you reach 70 or 80, things are getting risky. If you hit 100 (.10 BA), you are clearly at serious risk whether drinking or driving a car.

We want to make it clear that our moderate BA goal of 55 is not some arbitrary number picked out of a hat or selected because it nicely matches an easily remembered speed limit. There are various reasons why alcohol researchers generally agree that 50–55 is the moderate limit (see Appendix). Briefly they include:

   A. The good feelings produced by alcohol decrease above a BA of 55 for most drinkers.
   B. Impairment of physical functioning such as coordination accelerates above 55, along with the risk of all sorts of accidents.
   C. The negative effects on physical health are considered greater above that level.
   D. Emotional control becomes more unpredictable above 55.
   E. Stress relief ends above 55 for most drinkers, and more alcohol tends to increase anxiety rather than to reduce it.
   F. Hangovers occur mainly at BAs over 55, with their attendant negative effects on job performance, family, etc.

We must acknowledge that there are indeed some reasonably successful moderate drinkers who exceed the 55 limit yet suffer few harmful effects. However, in general we think 55 is the most sensible limit for successful drinking.

For the effects of various blood alcohol levels on behavior, see the chart below:

Blood Alcohol	Behavioral Effects
20	Mellow feeling beginning, less inhibited, slight body warmth
50	Definite relaxation, lowered alertness, driving somewhat impaired
100	Driving quite impaired, talkative, noisy, uninhibited, possible emotional or embarrassing behavior
150	Intoxication obvious in body movements, speech, emotional and mental behavior, and driving abilities
300	Extremely drunk
500	Probably fatal

With blood alcohol level being such an important influence on behavior, we need to consider just how alcohol gets into the body and what it does. When liquor is swallowed, the alcohol in it is absorbed rapidly through the stomach and the walls of the small intestines. The *rate* of absorption and resultant BA are determined by several factors, as shown in the chart below:

FAST ABSORPTION—RAPID AND HIGHER BLOOD ALCOHOL PEAK	SLOW ABSORPTION— DELAYED AND LOWER BLOOD ALCOHOL PEAK
Fast drinking—gulps	Slow drinking—sips
Straight drinks—little or no mixer	Mixed drinks—lots of mixer
Empty stomach	Full stomach
High-proof liquor	Low-proof liquor
Sugarless drinks	Sugar, fats, or milk in mixer

Rapid drinking is naturally associated with rapid absorption. Large amounts of alcohol in the stomach are absorbed faster because alcohol contacts the stomach wall and intestines over a larger surface area. Absorption is also most rapid when the digestive system is empty. Two ounces of pure alcohol mixed with eight ounces of water on an empty stomach can put twice as much alcohol in the blood as is the case when some bread or potatoes were previously eaten. Also, the blood alcohol with the stomach empty would reach its highest point after about an hour, whereas with a full stomach it would take twice as long. Thus food in the stomach not only tends to lower the peak blood alcohol concentration but also delays the effects.

The type of food or beverage consumed also affects absorption rate. Beer and sweet wines, high in sugars and starches, result in lower blood alcohol readings than would an equivalent amount of alcohol taken with water. Along these same lines, diluted drinks naturally produce lower readings than stronger drinks. The fats contained in milk, cream, and other dairy products also tend to slow down the absorption rate because they do not dissolve in alcohol.

Once alcohol is in the bloodstream, it is rapidly distributed throughout the body. Most important, it is carried to the brain, where it influences behavior. A human brain contains over 10 billion brain cells. These microscopic cells work in concert to serve as master of mind and body. They give rise to all behavior and are responsible for every thought and act during every second of our lives. Without these cells functioning properly, we would be unable to process, store, and retrieve information about our experiences. Virtually all of our internal bodily organs are also controlled either directly by the brain through connecting nerve cells or indirectly by chemicals (hormones) which are produced and distributed by the brain. Alcohol changes our behavior because it markedly changes the chemistry and operation of our brain cells and nerve fibers. There are many theories attempting to explain how alcohol changes brain functioning. The brain must have certain chemicals, such as oxygen, in correct amounts to operate efficiently. It may be that alcohol somehow disrupts the brain cells' ability to use oxygen. The basic idea is that an energy-starved brain would produce inefficient behavior. Indeed, starving the brain for oxygen even for a few seconds can radically alter behavior and depress consciousness. Further support for this idea comes from the observation that the behavioral effects of alcohol are more pronounced at high altitudes where there is less oxygen.

Alcohol also affects the brain by killing brain cells when a person drinks excessively. This loss is small on the daily basis but becomes significant over a period of years because brain cells, unlike other cells in our bodies, are not replaced. Therefore, alcohol damage to the brain over time is permanent. With heavy drinking, the impairment may become quite visible through undesired behavioral changes such as violent temper or memory loss. The classic "skid-row bum" is a tragic figure in part because his brain often is so damaged that no amount of rehabilitation can possibly restore him to normal brain functioning.

Recent research has indicated that alcohol may also disrupt the brain cells' ability to build proteins, the very "fabric of memory." Alcohol would thus impair the capacity for new learning and the ability to remember what has been experienced. Studies using intoxicated mice seem to confirm this theory.

Whatever the mechanism, it is clear that alcohol changes the chemical operation of brain cells. In addition, it tends to affect some brain cells before others. Technically, alcohol acts very much like a general anesthetic such as ether. First, it depresses our higher brain functions controlling vision, feeling, hearing, speech, thinking, attention, and movement. Soon afterwards, alcohol begins to depress or slow our lower brain centers which control vital functions such as breathing, heart rate, and sleep. Alcohol, unlike ether, is a poor surgical anesthetic because the amount required for loss of consciousness and elimination of pain is very close to that which produces death from overdose. Along these lines, it is important to note that barbiturates should never be mixed with alcohol. Sleeping pills or "downers," as they are often called, such as chloral hydrate, Doriden, Nembutal, phenobarbital, and Seconal act somewhat differently from alcohol, but in the end produce the same depression of the lower brain centers. The "drug summation" that occurs when alcohol and the barbiturate drugs ("reds") are mixed can be, and often is, fatal.

Anyone who has ever downed one too many knows what a hangover is—headache, nausea, irritability, dehydration, disorientation, and confusion. Some of these symptoms appear to result from the loss of a special dream sleep (Rapid Eye Movement or REM sleep) which normally takes up about 25 percent of all sleep. The abuser may get plenty of sleep but not the right *kind* of sleep, and the result can be the confusion, disorientation, irritability, and lethargy so familiar to hangover victims. Despite a rich folklore, the only certain way to *prevent* a hangover is to avoid drinking too much in the first place. It is a simple fact that the higher the BA and the greater the total amount consumed, the worse the hangover.

Hangovers are a little more likely to occur with some alcoholic beverages than with others. Those beverages highest in the impurities that produce flavor (congeners) are more likely also to produce a hangover or make it a bit worse. Beverages like bourbon or dark rum, which are high in flavor (and thus in congeners), are more likely to produce hangover symptoms than are beverages with less flavor, like gin or vodka. In general, the less color and taste, the lower the congener content and the less the likelihood of symptoms of headache and dehydration. Listed below are examples of the congener content of some popular brands of alcoholic beverages.

You can see that while vodka and gin have only slightly more congener content than neutral spirits ("pure" alcohol), the highly fla-

CONGENER CONTENT OF ALCOHOLIC BEVERAGES

(mg/100 ml at 100 proof)

	Totals
Grain neutral spirits	3.2
Smirnoff vodka	3.3
Gordon's gin	4.4
Seagram's VO whiskey	46.5
Bacardi Silver L. rum	60.1
Cutty Sark whisky	110.4
Seagram 7 Crown whiskey	130.6
Hennessy cognac	252.3
Old Crow whiskey	285.6

SOURCE: Carroll, 1972.

vored beverages like cognac are much higher in congener content. Often there will be significant differences between brands of the same kind of liquor as well. One brand of Scotch whiskey may be much higher or lower than another brand (perhaps distillers should include this information on the label). At any rate low-congener beverages may make a small difference in a hangover, but the effects are minor when compared to the amount consumed. Perhaps the basis for the popular notion that mixing various alcoholic beverages causes worse hangovers is that doing so results in a greater variety of congeners.

The only *cure* for a hangover is time and rest. Aspirin and antacids may relieve some of the discomfort, and folk medicine suggests many other remedies (such as a glass of salted cucumber juice in Russia or heavy cream in Norway), but none has good evidence to support it. The "hair-of-the-dog" remedy, more alcohol, may give a brief respite, but the net effect is to make things worse. Some have suggested drinking lots of water to prevent dehydration, staying up for an hour or two after drinking and before retiring, and taking doses of vitamins, but objective evidence evaluating these remedies is not available.

Relatively speaking, hangovers are distant in time from actual consumption, and so they generally fail to change one's drinking habits. The immediate effects of alcohol consumption in amounts large enough to cause a hangover can be both pleasant and unpleasant. The physical effects can include feelings of warmth and muscle relaxation, numbness and pressure, heaviness, blurring of vision, deeper and slower breathing, but also burning and irritation in the stomach, some loss of coordination, a dry mouth, and a flushed appearance. Usually the pleasant physical effects occur at relatively low blood alcohol concentrations. Increased consumption eventually results in various kinds of physical distress. One of the clear signs that someone is a current or potential alcohol abuser is the inability to feel the pleasant effects of intoxication after a drink or two.

When we drink and the alcohol circulates throughout the body and brain, it is slowly being decomposed or expelled from the body. Up to 5 percent is passed out in the urine; another 5 percent is exhaled from the lungs as the blood supply discharges waste products and takes on more oxygen. The liver is responsible for the breakdown or metabolism of the remaining 90 percent of the alcohol. The liver has limits to the amount of alcohol it can decompose in a given time period, processing about one drink per hour (1¼ ounces of whiskey, one beer, or 4 ounces of table wine). Alcohol causes the gradual buildup of fatty deposits in the liver and makes the liver less efficient in eliminating body wastes. This damage can eventually cause failure of the liver. When the body is unable to remove waste it becomes poisoned or polluted. This condition is commonly known as cirrhosis of the liver and can result in a most unpleasant death. It was once thought that cirrhosis in the heavy drinker was the result of poor eating habits and nutrition. More recent work indicates that it occurs even with a more than adequate diet.

Perhaps the most obvious health problems associated with alcohol consumption are unwanted pounds and poor nutrition. Alcohol has a very high number of calories per ounce compared to other beverages and often produces noticeable weight gain. Excessive weight has been clearly associated with heart and circulatory disease (in addition to alcohol's direct effect of decreasing the strength of heart muscle). If you calculate the number of calories in a bottle of beer (about 150) times the number of bottles consumed by some beer drinkers, it becomes clear that the "beer belly" is no accident. In fact, many excessive beer drinkers may be consuming more calories per day in beer than in food. This is serious when we realize that calories in alcohol are not accompanied by vitamins, minerals, and proteins. These empty calories do not have much food value. For some reason, possibly the high calorie content of alcohol, excessive drinkers often tend not to eat as much of the foods necessary to maintain good nutrition and health. Also, it is known that the excessive consumption of alcohol over a prolonged period of time damages the lining of the intestines and decreases their ability to absorb some sugars, some amino acids, vitamin B_{12}, and a number of other substances required for good health. The physical condition of the excessive drinker can be rapidly impaired when all of these factors work together. If an abusive drinker fails to eat properly, drinks many calories that have little food value, and also has intestinal damage so that food eaten cannot be used by the body, the resulting dietary deficiency tends to increase susceptibility to a variety of diseases and complicates the recovery from such disorders. Alcohol also disrupts the water balance of the body. Anyone who has ever consumed an excess of alcohol and experienced a dry mouth the next day can vouch for this fact. Low blood sugar, or hypoglycemia, also results from drinking and is one of the symptoms of hangover.

Other bodily effects associated with drinking are high blood pressure (hypertension), slightly increased heart rate but decreased pumping strength and efficiency (reduced cardiac output), and lowered testosterone (sex hormone) levels in males. We should not pass by a discussion of the effects of alcohol on the body without mentioning the Fetal Alcohol Syndrome, the sad reality for pregnant women that drinking even moderate amounts (2 or 3 drinks per day) can result in babies afflicted by mental retardation and a variety of physical abnormalities. The effects of alcohol are worse than the effects of tobacco on the growing fetus. Since nobody really knows how small an amount of alcohol or nicotine is sufficient to harm a growing fetus, the only rational advice for pregnant women is not to drink or smoke at all.

In summary, although light or moderate alcohol use may be physically and psychologically harmless and perhaps even beneficial, it is clear that *heavy* alcohol intake is connected with a variety of physical and behavioral ills and in the long run exacts a price well beyond what most of us would be willing to pay if we carefully considered the consequences.

Many people falsely believe that the effects of alcohol on the body and behavior can be decreased by taking some other drug such as the caffeine in coffee (as often suggested in TV shows and movies). However, no stimulant has ever been found that makes a drinker's judgment, perception, or conscious processes more normal, even though a sleepy drinking driver may become temporarily slightly more alert after a few cups of strong coffee—perhaps just long enough to get out on the highway. A coffee-filled drunk is still as drunk! Interpreting temporarily increased awareness as a greater degree of sobriety has probably killed thousands. Even food will not eliminate or dilute the alcohol already in the bloodstream. It will only slow the rate of alcohol absorption from the stomach and intestines into the blood. Vigorous physical activity has no effect on the elimination of alcohol in the blood, so you can't "sweat it out" either.

To determine the amount of alcohol affecting our bodies at any given time, we have to understand alcohol content in the beverages we drink. The strength of an alcoholic beverage is printed on the bottle label, either as "percent alcohol" or as "proof." The term "proof" came from a British Army procedure used to gauge the alcoholic content of distilled spirits. The liquid was poured over gunpowder and ignited. If the alcohol concentration was high enough, the gunpowder would go off with a "poof" and explode. That was proof that the beverage had an acceptable alcohol content, about 57 percent. Even though combustion is no longer used to test liquor, we have retained the term "proof." The actual percent of alcohol in a bottle is the proof divided by two. So, 80-proof whiskey contains 40-percent alcohol. By the same reasoning, a drink containing 100 percent or pure alcohol would be 200 proof.

Although alcoholic beverage manufacturers are required to state on the package the percentage of alcohol either directly or in terms of proof, a conspicuous and, we believe, unwise exception is made

Beverage	Percent Alcohol
Beer	4%
Ale	5%
Malt liquor	7%
Table (dry) wine (e.g., Burgundy and Chablis)	12%
Fortified (sweet) wine (e.g., sherry and port)	20%
Liqueurs (e.g., crème de menthe, Kahlua)	28%
Liquor (bourbon, brandy, Scotch, gin, vodka, etc.—80 proof)	40%

for the brewers of beer, ale, and malt liquors. Very few people know, for example, that there is more alcohol in one 12-ounce beer (4 percent or 0.48 ounce alcohol) than in one ounce of 80-proof liquor (40 percent of 1 ounce = 0.40 ounce alcohol). If you are trying honestly to keep track of your intake, it is essential to know how much alcohol is in different beverages. Above we have listed the more common forms of alcoholic beverages and the most common percent of alcohol in each.

Throughout this book we will consider beer to be 4 percent alcohol, table wine 12 percent alcohol, fortified wine 20 percent, and liquor 40 percent. Although different beers and wines may vary slightly from these figures, these are simply the most common percentages so we will use them for comparison with other alcoholic beverages. Some liquors, we realize, contain more than 40 percent alcohol, but there is a trend among distillers to produce more and more liquor at 40 percent (80 proof) and less at higher alcoholic percentages, so we will use 40 percent.

Most shot glasses measure 1 to 1½ ounces, with an average of about *1¼ ounces,* which we will use for our *standard liquor "drink" in this book.* With these assumptions in mind, we can now make some easily remembered "drink" comparisons:

APPROXIMATE "DRINK" EQUIVALENTS

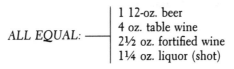

ALL EQUAL:
- 1 12-oz. beer
- 4 oz. table wine
- 2½ oz. fortified wine
- 1¼ oz. liquor (shot)

DRINK CONVERSION TABLE

Conversion of Wine to "Drinks"		Conversion of 80-Proof Liquor to "Drinks"	
Ounces of Wine	Number of Drinks*	Ounces of 80-Proof Liquor	Number of Drinks†
2	½	1	1
4	1	2	1½
6	1½	3	2½
8	2	4	3
10	2½	5	4
12	3	6	5
14	3½	7	5½
16	4	8	6½
18	4½	9	7
20	5	10	8
22	5½	11	9
24	6	12	9½
26	6½	13	10½
28	7	14	11
30	7½	15	12
32	8		
34	8½		
36	9		
38	9½		
40	10		

*4 ounces of wine (12% table wine) = 1 drink.
†1¼ ounces of 80-proof liquor = 1 drink.

If you are curious about how these equivalents were calculated, our standard "drink" containing about ½ ounce of pure alcohol was determined as follows:

4% of 12 oz. of beer = .48 oz. alcohol
12% of 4 oz. of table wine = .48 oz. alcohol
20% of 2½ oz. of fortified wine = .50 oz. alcohol
40% of 1¼ oz. of liquor = .50 oz. alcohol

Many drinkers have only a vague idea of how many drinks they've had at any given time, but counting drinks is very important. Keeping track of drinks is easy if you drink 12-ounce beers—just add up the number of beers consumed. For 12 percent wine, just divide the total number of ounces by 4 to get the number of drinks or see the table opposite. If you use a 1¼-ounce shot glass for liquor (which we, recommend), it's easy too. Simply count the number of shots you poured and that's how many drinks you had. Bar drinks can be assumed to be 1¼ ounce unless you know otherwise. If you prefer to count total ounces of liquor, then divide by 1¼ to get drinks, or simply look at the table shown on page 42 (tables are also included with BA tables at the back of the book).

It takes a little figuring if you drink more than one kind of alcoholic beverage. For example, if you drank two cocktails (1¼ ounces each of bourbon) before dinner and three 4-ounce glasses of wine with dinner, how many "drinks" would you have consumed?

Two 1¼-oz. cocktails	= 2	drinks
Three 4-oz. glasses of table wine	= 3	drinks
	Total = 5	drinks

What if you drank three 1¼-ounce cocktails, had 14 ounces of table wine with dinner, then capped that off with 2 ounces of brandy?

Three 1¼-oz. cocktails	= 3	drinks
14 oz. table wine at 4 oz. per drink	= 3½	drinks
2 oz. brandy	= 1½	drinks
	Total = 8	drinks

Knowing the number of "drinks" you have had and how much time it took to drink them is all you need to be able to determine your blood alcohol. You simply look up your BA in the tables at the end of the book, based upon your body weight. As in the first example, if you weigh 130 pounds and drink 5 drinks in two hours, you would look up your BA in this table:

130-Pound Person

Hours since start of drinking	Number of Drinks									
	1	2	3	4	5	6	7	8	9	10
1	15	40	70	95	125	150	180	205	235	260
2	0	25	55	80	110	135	165	190	220	245
3	0	10	40	65	95	120	150	175	205	230
4	0	0	25	50	80	105	135	160	190	215
5	0	0	10	35	65	90	120	145	175	200

As you can see, your BA would be 110.

If you weighed 180 pounds and drank the 8 drinks in the second example in four hours, your BA would be 100 (see tables at the end of the book).

Whether you are male or female makes a very small difference in BA. Women will have slightly higher BAs than men of the same weight when they drink identical amounts. But for practical purposes the difference is not enough to be concerned about and does not affect the use of the BA tables.

Other factors besides BA influence behavior, including physical condition, previous drinking experience, level of fatigue, and the social environment. But because it is easy to do, it is customary for researchers or police to determine intoxication simply by measuring blood alcohol through tests of blood, urine, or breath. Blood and urine tests used to be considered the most reliable measures of blood alcohol, but they are less preferred today because they are messy, inconvenient, and sometimes present technical problems of accuracy. The amount of alcohol in the blood is not equally distributed throughout the body, a higher concentration usually being found in the trunk with less in the limbs and fingers. Therefore, while a simple blood sample taken from the finger may be convenient, it is not so highly correlated as is a breath sample with the actual blood alcohol concentration in the *brain* (which is most important in affecting behavior).

Breath-measuring devices have in recent years become quite reliable in making indirect blood alcohol measurements. The proportion of alcohol in the breath stays in a constant relationship to the concentration of alcohol in the central blood supply. Therefore, the reading displayed on a breath-analysis machine is an excellent if indirect estimate of the blood alcohol concentration.

Remember, once alcohol is in the blood, it takes *time* to be eliminated. The body can burn off (metabolize) about one drink in an hour (15 BA units), so to the extent you drink faster than this, alcohol is going to build up. Three drinks per hour over a period of two hours (6 drinks) would mean that at the end of the second hour you would have 4 drinks in your body and it would take about four hours more until they burn off and you are completely sober. The faster you drink, the more your body gets behind, and the longer it will take to metabolize the alcohol remaining in your blood.

In summary, the main factors affecting blood alcohol are physical size, stomach contents, condition of health, drinking rate, and beverage concentration.

YOU ARE WHAT YOU DRINK

Some people claim "you are what you eat." It's certainly also true that you are what you drink! Here is a tongue-in-cheek description of what you are likely to be as your BA increases:

> At 20, *dynamic and delightful*
> At 40, *dashing and debonair*
> At 70, *dull and dopey*
> At 100, *dizzy and disturbing*
> At 150, *disoriented and disgusting*
> At 200, *debilitated and despicable*
> At 250, *delirious and dangerous*
> At 300, *dead drunk*
> At 500, *dead*

4

Jekyll and Hyde

Senator Howard Baker tells of a Congressman receiving a very brief letter. It simply said, "Dear Congressman, how do you stand on whiskey?" Not knowing whether his correspondent was for whiskey or against whiskey, the Congressman framed the following reply:

My dear friend:

I had not intended to discuss this controversial subject at this particular time. However, I want you to know that I do not shun a controversy. On the contrary, I will take a stand on any issue at any time, regardless of how fraught with controversy it may be. You have asked me how I feel about whiskey. Here is how I stand on this issue.

If, when you say whiskey, you mean the Devil's brew; the poison scourge; the bloody monster that defiles innocence, dethrones reason, destroys the home, creates misery, poverty, fear, literally takes the bread from the mouths of little children; if you mean the evil drink that topples the Christian man and woman from the pinnacles of righteous, gracious living into the bottomless pit of degradation and despair, shame and helplessness and hopelessness, then certainly, I am against it with all of my power.

But, if when you say whiskey, you mean the oil of conversation, the philosophic wine, the ale that is consumed when great fellows get together, that puts a song in their hearts and laughter on their lips, and the warm glow of contentment in their eyes; if you mean Christmas cheer; if you mean the stimulating drink that puts the spring in the old gentleman's step on a frosty morning; if you mean the drink that enables the man to magnify his joy and his happiness and to forget, if only for a little while, life's great tragedies and heartbreaks and sorrows. If you mean that drink the sale of which pours into our Treasury untold millions of dollars which are used to provide tender care for little crippled children, our blind, our deaf, our pitiful aged and infirm; to build highways, hospitals and schools, then certainly I am in favor of it.

This is my stand, and I will not compromise.

Your Congressman

Senator Baker comments that the humor in the Congressman's reply stems from its documentation as a feat of fence-straddling of heroic proportions. He also notes that the attitudes expressed encompass the most common rationalizations and attacks that have become a part of the American experience with alcohol.

Alcohol *is* the dominant drug in this country today. The laws, attractive advertising, relatively low cost, and the availability of alcohol have helped to make it a $20-billion-a-year habit. The huge tax revenue from this enterprise contributes significantly to our national economy. It should be apparent that thousands of jobs are connected with the production, distribution, and sale of alcoholic beverages. From the farmers who grow the grapes, grain, hops, barley, rye, and even potatoes (used in vodka), to the bartenders and cocktail waitresses who serve drinks in clubs, a multitude of people have their personal financial security tied to the consumption of alcohol. The true economic benefits to society of alcohol production and consumption are impossible to assess, but they are unquestionably great. (Whether or not they outweigh the *costs* is another question.)

Of course, most of us do not drink to keep someone else in a job. We drink because of what we personally experience with alcohol. While the following discussion should not be seen as an effort to romanticize drinking or to promote it as a great and wonderful thing to do, we must recognize that drinking is popular because it *enhances* most drinkers' lives, and does so in a variety of ways.

For some drinkers, the enjoyment of flavor alone is sufficient reason to partake of wine, beer, creative mixed drinks, liqueurs, or whatever strikes their fancy. Anyone who has enjoyed a visit to the beautiful Napa Valley wine country in California, sampling the various wines in rustic tasting rooms, has partaken of a memorable esthetic experience. Fine liquor has traditionally been enjoyed with fine food, enhancing the appreciation and enjoyment of delicate flavors and aromas.

Some physicians recommend what many drinkers have known for centuries: A little wine at mealtime helps the digestion. Many hospitals now offer a glass of wine with meals. It also appears that alcohol in moderation may increase our bodily health, aiding circulation as suggested by Kozararevic's work. Light drinkers may live longer than people who do not drink at all (see the *Second Special Report to the U.S. Congress on Alcohol and Health*).

Alcohol is often called a social lubricant because many people *do* feel more comfortable in social situations with the help of the relaxation provided by a drink or two. The alcohol "glow" tends to highlight special occasions, making already happy people feel even better, adding sparkle to conversation and laughter to the air. Alcohol seems to help us tune out of today's troubles as well as be less troubled by our worries about tomorrow. It aids our focus on the here and now so we can savor the good things of life, from food to friends, at a richer level of enjoyment.

For many drinkers, the consumption of alcohol provides a pleasant altered state of consciousness and bodily feelings. These changes may be a welcome contrast to the intense and busy activities of the workaday world. Alcohol provides a break, a brief interlude in experience that, for many, makes it easier to return later to battle with the dragons of everyday life.

All of these positive aspects of drinking are the Dr. Jekyll side of alcohol, the "good" face of what can, as we all know, be a dangerously two-faced creature. The Mr. Hyde side is the ugly reality that alcohol is the modern world's most serious drug problem. As noted earlier, over 70 percent of the adult American population drink and, although nearly 40 percent drink regularly, most of them drink sensibly. These drinkers are not the core of the problem. Current studies suggest that about 7 percent of the American population have serious problems with alcohol (over 15 million people). In terms of misuse, then, alcohol presents a far greater social problem than *all other drugs combined.* A great deal of concern in recent years over the "youth drug culture" has directed our attention away from one very important fact: for every young person with a serious illegal drug problem, there are *several dozen adults* with equally serious alcohol problems.

What is meant by an "alcohol problem"? Millions of people drink alcohol excessively and yet would not necessarily be considered what some call "alcoholics." Generally speaking, an alcohol problem exists when the use of alcohol restricts the drinker's lifestyle, limits potential, or damages health. An alcohol problem also exists when a drinker's behavior interferes with the lifestyle, potential, or health of *other persons* with whom he or she associates. Tragically, the first relationships to be damaged are often those involving the most significant persons in our lives. Our loved ones, close friends, and even neighbors usually are alienated long before our more distant relationships become strained.

Alcohol is also associated with various social problems including violence, crime, poor job performance, auto accidents, child and spouse abuse, and suicide. The behavior of the abuser can affect the quality of life of countless other people.

Before we consider reasons for excessive drinking, it will be helpful to identify the basic ways people relate to alcohol. Many categories have been used to classify drinkers. Our approach is to be as practical and realistic as possible. We propose three basic groups: *nondrinkers* (abstainers), *successful drinkers,* and *unsuccessful drinkers.* Nondrinkers, of course, are easy to identify—they never drink. But we need some measuring devices for carefully considering successful and unsuccessful drinkers. The best yardsticks we have found are *amount and frequency of consumption, typical blood alcohol level,* and the *consequences of drinking* (social, economic, marital, physical, vocational, legal, and personal).

Successful drinkers usually do not drink every day, nor do they drink for more than an hour or so at a sitting. The amount, which can vary quite a bit depending on body weight, is usually 1 to 4 drinks of average size (12-ounce beer, 1¼ ounce of hard liquor, 4 ounces of table wine). The larger the body, of course, the more they can consume and remain below a moderate blood alcohol level of 55. In terms of consequences from drinking, successful drinkers typically enjoy their social contacts with or without alcohol. They suffer no economic liabilities from their drinking and it is not a problem in their marriage or other important relationships. Alcohol has not caused any physical problems for successful drinkers, and their job performance is unaffected by drinking. They have never been arrested for a drinking-related offense and, of course, they don't worry that alcohol is hurting them in any way. Their bodies have not adapted (built up tolerance) to the effects of alcohol. In addition, alcohol is not used to handle serious stress or escape from important problems. Rather, they tend to deal with personal problems directly, seldom resorting to alcohol for help. Lest this angelic description unfairly exclude you as a successful drinker, we should also note that many successful drinkers *do* once in a great while drink too much. Many successful drinkers become somewhat intoxicated perhaps three or four times a year, such as on New Year's Eve, their birthday, or some other special holiday. However, when intoxicated, successful drinkers do not risk the welfare of others by driving or attempting other important responsible actions. Insofar as a drinker's behavior is not harmful to others even though he might drink to excess, we regard such a drinker as less problematic.

Unsuccessful drinking or "abuse" is a matter of degree. Many abusers drink every day. Those who do not drink daily still tend to overdo it when they do drink and their behavior shows it. Or they may drink moderately on several occasions and then, quite unpredictably, drink far too much the next time. Daily abusers tend to deal with the natural problems of living by regularly resorting to alcohol, and after some time their drinking begins to *add to* their stresses rather than reduce them.

Some researchers believe that the fundamental difference between the unsuccessful and the successful social drinker may be seen in the *way* they drink. The question is an open one at this point, but it has been observed that alcohol abusers tend to rapidly consume straight or strong drinks in gulps, quickly abandoning any intention to limit their drinking. The successful drinker prefers to sip a more diluted, mixed drink over a longer period of time and tends to retain control so that he or she rarely, if ever, gets drunk.

Alcohol abusers' blood alcohol can range anywhere from 50 to 300 or even higher, depending upon how they drink. Some of them maintain a fairly low BA, but stay there for many hours or even days. Others drink faster and reach very high blood alcohol levels. The higher the BA, and the longer a BA is maintained, the worse the consequences. The number and seriousness of the consequences are also good measures of degree of abuse.

The case of Mark, presented in Chapter 1, is an example of a moderate abuser. Less serious abusers than Mark do not drink as much or regularly reach a BA of 110 as he does, nor have they typically had his legal problems or vocational, marital, or personal concerns caused by drinking. Also, milder abusers probably don't worry about their drinking as much as Mark. More serious abusers than Mark have greater intakes with higher BAs and more severe consequences. They may be very restricted socially, going only to drinking events with other heavy drinkers, and may be burdened with considerable expense for booze, perhaps legal problems, and loss of income from missing work. They may end up divorced, suffering from physical ailments, and in anguish over not being able to control their drinking habit.

Having briefly examined types of drinkers (to which we will return later), let's look at the reasons behind different kinds of drinking habits. Some of the factors which influence how people drink are:

1. Rules for drinking in their culture
2. Parental and peer drinking
3. The effectiveness of their social skills for meeting needs
4. The number and effectiveness of satisfying alternatives to drinking
5. Biological reaction to alcohol
6. The body's acquired tolerance to the effects of alcohol
7. Methods of handling stress

Cultural rules and drinking were discussed in Chapter 2. Briefly, we know that people tend to adopt drinking patterns that are acceptable to their cultural group. The availability of alcohol and the media's portrayal of the role of alcohol in people's lives are strong influences. A major factor is the drinking habits of one's parents. Heavy- or moderate-drinking parents teach by demonstration. Teetotalers tend to have children who do not drink at all or who, because they have no real-life models for appropriate drinking, tend to drink *too* much (more so than children of moderate-drinking parents). Peers naturally begin to influence drinking during the teenage years and can also become very powerful influences.

People who have learned to understand others and be self-sufficient tend to rely less on alcohol to help them in social interactions. For example, they can be assertive and appropriate in approaching members of the opposite sex *while sober*, whereas unsuccessful drinkers need a couple of drinks first. People who enjoy a rich variety of pleasurable activities such as socializing, relaxing, or playing also tend not to use alcohol as much.

Inborn biological factors may influence drinking in that some individuals seem to experience a greater effect from alcohol and to suffer less from hangovers. Adaptation to the effects of alcohol is also a factor that can affect anyone who drinks regularly. Regular (especially daily) drinkers often find that their customary amount may not be producing the same effects as before, so they have to drink more to get the same high. Over time, their drinking may gradually increase.

How people handle everyday stress influences drinking and has historically been given a great deal of attention. Most of us would probably agree that modern life inevitably includes a variety of conflicts, fears, frustrations, anxieties, and even boredom. (Life certainly has its good points too, but we're not upset by them.) A basic challenge in day-to-day living, then, is to continue to function effectively with some degree of overall satisfaction in the face of major and minor stresses. It is not a new idea to connect alcohol abuse with attempts to handle stress. We should note, however, that stress is an inevitable feature of life, a perfectly natural part of living in a stimulating world. There is a widely held belief that the ideal life might be a *stress-free* life, but in reality the only way to be truly stress-free is to be dead. (Getting married, raising children, being promoted, or traveling through Europe are all positive experiences, but are also "stressful.")

Like all living creatures, human beings engage in behavior designed to reduce undesired stress and keep life relatively stable. Some of us have learned that by enduring a little more stress in the short run, confronting and solving problems directly, we are better off in the long haul. When problem-solvers use alcohol, they tend to be successful drinkers and the hassles of daily life do not become tied up in any way with drinking. On the other hand, there are those who learn to incorporate alcohol into their lifestyle in an attempt to reduce stress and make day-to-day activities easier to cope with. Many drinkers use stress as an excuse to drink ("I wouldn't need to drink so much if I had a better job," or "I'd drink a lot less if my husband didn't criticize me so much"). But rarely are their problems solved since they typically are merely avoided or postponed. Usually the alcohol approach to reducing stress compounds old problems and leads to new ones. Such individuals rarely recognize the ineffectiveness of their "alcohol solution" to stress until matters have become quite serious.

The latest research indicates that alcohol reduces stress and anxiety up to a BA of about 55, but above 55 *actually increases anxiety!* Once again, moderation has benefits that excess destroys. And, of course, drinking makes no change in the conditions that cause stress, but gives only temporary relief.

Today it is considered simplistic to view *all* alcohol abuse as an attempt to reduce life's stresses. In fact, some heavy drinkers may actually find significance in life because of the attention that comes from their being deviant, and that attention can then serve to *increase* excessive drinking. This is why many counselors recommend that the spouses of abusers should not badger them about it.

The obvious conclusion is that abusive drinking is a complex problem with no simple explanation. We have discussed the meaning of alcohol abuse and looked at a variety of influences on individual drinking habits. We are convinced that there is always a *combination* of factors which determine how a person drinks. In our opinion, no one factor is critical. Successful drinkers tend to have moderate-drinking parents and good social skills, to engage in satisfying alternatives to drinking, and to have the ability to meet their needs and cope with stress. Abusers do not.

Thus there are many roads leading to the abuse of alcohol. We hope you have managed to avoid them. If not, don't give up—help is on the way. In the next chapter we will begin to describe our program for becoming a more successful drinker. The first step is observing the good and the bad things that happen when people drink.

PART II   How to Become a Successful Drinker

IN THIS SECTION we present a step-by-step program for changing drinking habits. The underlying rationale is that *many strategies dealing with various aspects of the drinking habit must be used together*. First, it is important to be keenly aware of how alcohol affects behavior for better or for worse. We suggest that you carefully observe the positive and negative effects of alcohol on others as they drink, as well as on yourself. You must evaluate your drinking and find out what you need to do about it. Determining your own drinking limit provides a personal goal for successful alcohol use. We explore the topic of how to enlist the aid of supportive friends and relatives to greatest advantage. To change well-established habits you must be highly motivated, so we provide strategies to prepare for and maintain the necessary effort. Handling situations where you drink too much is critical in avoiding the most troublesome obstacles to success. People who pressure you to drink beyond your limit must be held in check, and satisfying alternatives to drinking should be found to make it easier to limit your use of alcohol. Those who know how to relax without alcohol have no need to drink for this purpose, so we

55

describe a technique for relaxing at will. The more serious abusers who should quit drinking entirely are given special assistance in using those methods best suited to their needs. Finally, we summarize all of these methods and describe how they work together for successful drinking.

5

Drink Watching

Even though you have no doubt been exposed to drinking situations, chances are you have not observed drinkers' behavior in a systematic way that alerted you to the difference between "successful" and "unsuccessful" drinking (getting the good from drinking without the bad). We can learn a lot about the effects of alcohol by carefully watching others drink and also by paying attention to ourselves as we drink.

If you are a drinker, you have probably noticed that the biggest changes happen during the first half hour or so of drinking. The reason is that when you start sober and drink to a BA of 40 or 50, the contrast between sobriety and moderate intoxication is striking. Continuing to drink beyond a BA of 55 will not result in feeling better. On the contrary, most drinkers will feel worse and suffer greater physical and mental impairment to boot. For these reasons, the basic rule of successful and enjoyable drinking can be stated clearly: *savor the good effects as your blood alcohol is rising up to a maximum of 55 and then quit drinking.* The effects from drinking are not so positive once the peak BA is reached and maintained for 15 minutes or so, or goes above 55. And a falling BA never feels as good as a rising one. *The same BA when the BA is rising feels much better than it does when the BA is falling.* This is how alcohol affects our body. Alcohol researchers call it "acute tolerance" or "adaptation."

The effects of tolerance are easy to understand because they are part of everyone's experience. A good example is what happens when you enter a kitchen with a strong smell of garlic. At first your nose is fresh and sensitive so the garlic odor seems strong. But in a few minutes you may hardly notice it because your sense of smell has adapted or become tolerant to the odor. That is exactly the way our "alcohol sense" works. If you add more garlic to garlicky soup, you probably won't smell it much—but it may spoil the soup! Similarly, if you consume additional drinks when you're already at a BA of 55, you won't increase your good feelings but may spoil the fun of drinking on that occasion.

The chart below shows a typical relationship between BA and the accompanying feelings of intoxication as BA rises and falls over a five-hour period.

While the BA rises, feelings of intoxication rise at about the same rate. But when the BA begins to drop, it drops more slowly than the accompanying feeling of intoxication. In other words, for any given blood alcohol level, say 40, you feel more intoxicated when your BA is going up than when it is coming down. Once you have stopped drinking, and your BA is declining, you will feel sober well before your BA would indicate true sobriety. Your body has become tolerant to alcohol. Most drinkers *feel* sober when their BA has dropped

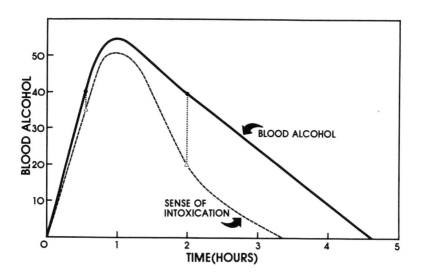

to between 20 and 30. Those who drink above 55 will feel sober at correspondingly higher BAs on the way down. The result is that even if you feel sober, your ability to perform complicated tasks, like driving, is still being affected. Physical coordination, and especially the ability to react to emergencies, depends more on the actual BA than on your feelings of intoxication or sobriety. Therefore, you must remember that even if you feel sober, your coordination may be impaired and you should not drive or attempt other complex and dangerous tasks until your actual BA has declined to the point of sobriety.

In summary, since a BA above 55 loses its positive quality for most drinkers, and a rising BA feels much better than a falling BA, we can conclude that the most satisfying and successful way to drink is to start completely sober, drink for 30–45 minutes up to a maximum BA of 55, stay there for 15–30 minutes, and then come back down. That's the ideal, anyway, since booze just doesn't offer really good highs for more than an hour or so. Pay attention to this simple rule and you will be miles ahead of most drinkers in your responsible enjoyment of alcohol. Drinking for longer periods of time can, of course, be enjoyable, but most drinkers in our research report it to be less and less of a positive experience as the drinking period increases. The law of diminishing returns applies to drinking.

AN EXERCISE: OBSERVE A DRINKER

We would like to suggest an exercise for you, whether you are a drinker or not: Systematically observe someone drink. It will be both amusing and valuable. During the cocktail hour, at a party, or simply at home with your spouse or friends, take careful note of the changes in a drinker's mood, thinking, coordination, and social skills as the drinker goes from completely sober to somewhat intoxicated. As a general guideline, in an hour a 150-pound person will reach a BA of 55 after drinking 3 beers, 2 to 3 mixed drinks (depending on how strong they are), or about 12 ounces of wine.

Mentally, gather samples of the drinker's behavior at different times. Try to interact with the person you are watching *before* drinking begins or at least before he or she has had very much of the first drink. You, of course, should be slowly nursing a drink or sipping a nonalcoholic beverage so that you can see things as they really are. Try to have repeated contact with your drinker at various intoxication levels.

RITA TRIES OBSERVATION

Rita, one of our clients, recently agreed to see if she could really focus upon changes in people at an office party. Her friend and coworker, Rob, was a sensible drinker most of the time but at parties tended to overdo it a bit. Rita figured the party would provide a good opportunity to watch Rob and see whether or not he became less pleasant and seemed to have less fun above 55 BA. Rob weighs about 180 pounds, so Rita estimated that three or four drinks would be his moderate limit. True to form, early in the party Rob was talkative and witty, laughed a lot, and was reasonably polite. After his fourth drink, however, he began to make sarcastic comments and became sloppy, then seemed depressed, surly, and rather withdrawn. Rita had never noticed these changes so clearly before, even though she had known Rob for ten years and had seen him at many drinking occasions.

When watching someone drink, what you will most likely see is the drinker becoming relaxed and a little less inhibited with the first drink. Drinkers often express their feelings more and "let go" of their usual worries and concerns. Two drinks will increase these tendencies and often make them more talkative. Usually these changes in mood and behavior will seem positive (assuming the drinker is not dealing with a big personal problem at the time and does not have serious personality hang-ups such as being unable to express frustration or anger when sober). Keep track of how much he drinks. The full effects of each drink usually occur about 20 minutes after it is finished. About 20 minutes after the third drink (or the number of drinks it takes to exceed 55) you should begin to notice some negative effects and fewer positive ones. For example, you may see exaggerated emotions including unpleasant ones, loss of physical coordination and speech to some degree, and thought impairments such as memory problems or forgetting where they are in the middle of a sentence. Sloppiness, such as spilling drinks, and social unpleasantness (insults, sarcasm, inappropriate cursing, slurs) occur with many people. Instead of being happy and animated, they may become reserved, depressed, or aggressive. Individual reactions vary greatly, but this basic change from positive to negative usually occurs. The main exception is when a drinker habitually drinks above 55 and is therefore not very sensitive to lower BA levels. Such a drinker won't show as much change until his BA is already excessive—that is, above 55. Sometimes people with personal problems who use alcohol to get relief also react differently from normal drinkers and may not show the expected effect.

If the people you are watching stop drinking around a BA of 40 to 50, you will see that they continue to feel good for a half hour or so because their blood alcohol is still rising as more alcohol is absorbed into their blood. But after 20 to 30 minutes the positive effects will begin to decrease. On the other hand, they won't usually show the negative effects of someone who drinks to higher BAs. The positive effects will simply decrease. As we will explain later, this period of declining BA is an ideal time to do something enjoyable such as eat, read, watch TV, or go to bed.

If you will pay attention to some drinkers, make your observations, and keep track of behavior, you will observe what we have described. The good effects from drinking predominantly occur from a zero BA to about 55.

As noted above, one sign of alcohol abuse is when drinkers feel very little effect from alcohol at moderate BA levels. They have developed chronic *tolerance*. They are less sensitive overall to the effects of alcohol than most people because they have consumed so much more alcohol in the past. Since people often drink to experience pleasant changes in their feelings, if they fail to get them at moderate BA levels they will be prone to drink more than they should. Research demonstrates clearly that alcohol abusers have to drink more just to feel *as good as* successful drinkers do.

JESSE

In our research some years ago we wanted to see how well we could teach abusers to estimate their BA. We gave them drinks and periodically asked them to score their feelings and estimate their BA, which we then checked on our BA machine. The idea was to help them more clearly associate their growing feelings of intoxication with their BA so they could successfully slow down or stop as they approached a moderate BA level. Jesse volunteered to try the training, but after 3, then 4, and still more drinks—until his BA was over 80—he felt nothing at all! Jesse and other heavy drinkers taught us that we couldn't train people who have "burned out" their alcohol sense to estimate moderate BAs on the basis of their feelings of intoxication. They don't have any feelings at moderate levels! (Fortunately, most drinkers are not in that boat. Jesse had consumed nearly a quart of liquor every day for years.)

We should note that heavy drinkers will also *feel* sober sooner than successful drinkers even though they have a higher BA. This is one reason there are so many drunk drivers on the road—they *feel* sober but are actually still intoxicated and markedly impaired in their driving ability. You burn off only about one drink an hour, so if you have consumed 6 drinks in two hours, you will still have 4 of them in your body *regardless of how you feel.*

DETERMINING BLOOD ALCOHOL

To record necessary drinking information in an easy way, the concerned drinker should temporarily carry around a card such as that shown below, with columns for when, what, how many, how long, etc. Tally each drink *before the first sip* (when people try to do it later, they are less conscious of each drink, their memory is poor, or they forget to record them altogether). Note the type of liquor, time

Date_____	Drinking Occasions				
	Lunch	Cocktail hour	Dinner	Evening	Other
Mood (e.g., happy, satisfied, anxious, depressed)					
Reason for drinking (e.g., relax, socialize, tune out)					
Time Start					
Drink Type and Amount (e.g., 12 oz. beer, 1¼ oz. whiskey)					
Drink Proof					
Drink Tally					
Time End					
BA from Tables					

of day, and drinking conditions (place, people, situation). The conditions of drinking, such as mood and reason for drinking, are very important for identifying situations that are troublesome for the drinker. Situational information will also tell when the drinker is likely to drink successfully. Knowing a person's approximate weight, the number of drinks they had, and how long it took to drink them, we can look up their BA in the tables at the end of the book.

ANOTHER EXERCISE: OBSERVE YOURSELF

Now that you know how to estimate blood alcohol, you may want to take a closer look at yourself. If you are a drinker, one measure of your success is how sensitive *you* are to the effects of alcohol. So the next suggestion, *to watch yourself drink,* will be one test of your success with alcohol. Watching yourself drink will also help you become more aware of some of the effects that you may not normally notice.

Watching yourself is admittedly quite different from watching others drink. To be able to pay attention to your own behavior means you should not be distracted by others. You will need to find a time and place all to yourself without the likelihood of interruption and start completely sober. The Bodily Sensations Checklist below is easy to use and will help you focus upon your changing emotional and physical state. Fill it out first *before* you start drinking and then about 20 minutes after each drink to measure their effect. When you have finished your last drink, continue to mark the checklist every 20 minutes until you "feel" sober. (You can keep the ratings straight by using numbers or different marks each time.) Those who think this is too much trouble should at least compare a sober rating with one taken after the second or perhaps the third drink.

Indicate on each scale your state by marking the number that most closely describes your feeling at that moment:

BODILY SENSATIONS CHECKLIST

Euphoric (pleasant mood)

1	2	3	4	5	6	7
not at all						very much so

Relaxed

1	2	3	4	5	6	7
not at all						very much so

Tendency to Worry

1	2	3	4	5	6	7
not at all						very much so

Anxious

1	2	3	4	5	6	7
not at all						very much so

Talkative

1	2	3	4	5	6	7
not at all						very much so

Loud Voice
  1   2   3   4   5   6   7
not at all   very much so

Slurred Speech
  1   2   3   4   5   6   7
not at all   very much so

Warm, Flushed Face
  1   2   3   4   5   6   7
not at all   very much so

Impaired Vision (delayed fine-print focus)
  1   2   3   4   5   6   7
not at all   very much so

Impaired Balance (feet together, eyes closed, head tilted back)
  1   2   3   4   5   6   7
not at all   very much so

Coordination Impaired (walking heel to toe)
  1   2   3   4   5   6   7
not at all   very much so

Coordination/Eye-hand Impaired (touch each finger in sequence to thumb—back and forth rapidly)
  1   2   3   4   5   6   7
not at all   very much so

Dizzy
  1   2   3   4   5   6   7
not at all   very much so

Headachy
  1   2   3   4   5   6   7
not at all   very much so

Nauseated
  1   2   3   4   5   6   7
not at all   very much so

How Intoxicated Are You?
  1   2   3   4   5   6   7
not at all   very much so

Filling out and studying the checklist will help you to map out those changes that motivate you to drink in the first place (the positive changes that you experience when you drink). It will also help you detect at what level of blood alcohol those changes begin to decrease or lose some of their positive quality. Finally, becoming more sensitive to the varied effects of alcohol will help you to estimate your blood alcohol level.

Remember, a successful drinker knows and savors the good feelings that accompany moderate BA levels. If you feel almost nothing as your BA rises up to 40 or 50, you have probably dulled your alcohol sense from overdrinking in the past. You might even have to stop drinking altogether for a while in order to allow your body to become more sensitive to alcohol again. As we mentioned, being unable to clearly feel the effects of alcohol at lower BA levels is a bad sign. It means you have consumed too much for too long and your body has "burned out" from repeated exposure to too much alcohol, just as a bright light can temporarily blind you.

Whatever the case, try to be keenly aware of the effects as your BA is rising. Stop drinking after 2 or 3 drinks, or the number which you need to achieve a BA of 50 or 55. Pay careful attention to your feelings for 20 or 30 minutes *after* you stop drinking. You will continue to feel good if you are a successful drinker. After half an hour or so, though, your good feelings will decrease. Even if you have another drink, the *good* feelings will begin to decline. You just can't win because of the way our bodies are programmed to adapt. Unfortunately, most drinkers don't know this and assume that if a little makes them feel good, more will make them feel better, and a lot more will feel a lot better. Not so!

After you stop drinking, note how long it takes you to feel sober. Twenty minutes after your last drink your BA will reach its peak and will then drop by about 15 per hour. So if you reach 55, your BA will fall to 40 after one hour, 25 after two hours, 10 after three hours, and be at 0 again about three hours and forty minutes later. But most people will feel sober long before three hours and forty minutes are up.

On another drinking occasion, you might try drinking enough to bring your BA up to 70 or 80. Use your weight table at the end of the book to determine how much you would need to drink. For example, a 110-pound person would have to drink 2½ or 3 drinks in an hour to reach a BA of 70 to 80 (remember, only 1¼ ounces of hard liquor is a "drink"). A 220-pound person would need 5 or 6 drinks to get there. But *don't do this exercise if you are unaccustomed to drinking this much in an hour* because you will probably get sick. Do this only under safe and secure conditions such as at home in the evening with a sober spouse or friend present who knows what you are doing, has been with you before when you drank a lot, and has agreed to stay sober and watch after you.

Again, fill out the checklist before starting, then 20 minutes after each drink, and then after your last drink every 20 minutes until you "feel" sober. If you are not an abuser and therefore not tolerant to higher BA levels, you will notice that the good effects that motivated your drinking in the first place diminish above 55 and are gradually replaced by unpleasant feelings. Pay careful attention just as you did for the good effects up to 55, because you may not have noticed these unpleasant feelings before (while drinking, we often pay attention to other things and ignore these unpleasant sensations). Or, if you have noticed them, it may have been too late by then to do anything about it because earlier drinks were still not absorbed into the bloodstream. For example, you may be feeling great at 40. You got to 40 from the drink you finished 20 minutes before. But in the meantime you have already downed another because of the delay in effects and adaptation. The one you just drank will not take full effect for 20 or 30 more minutes and may put you over 55. *Drinking another drink before the effects from the last one have hit is one reason why many drinkers slip over the moderate level.* And frequently doing this increases the body's tolerance to the effects of alcohol, which further decreases sensitivity to moderate BA levels. The sensible conclusion, of course, is to wait long enough between drinks so that you have a chance to feel the last one before you start the next one. And remember, you get diminishing returns on your drinking anyway as your body adapts to the effects of alcohol.

The experience of watching yourself drink should help you become more aware of the changes produced by alcohol. It will also make it easier for you to enjoy the good without the bad and pave the way for more successful drinking.

If you have developed tolerance for alcohol, changing that tolerance will require a change in drinking habits. If you drink less often and reduce the amount, you will become more sensitive to alcohol after a while. Even one week of abstinence will increase your ability to enjoy alcohol. To begin learning how to drink less and enjoy it more, try quitting for a week or more. Or drink only twice a week, and then only to a BA of 30 or 40. Even breaking up a daily drinking pattern into every other day will help some.

To prevent tolerance from creeping back once you have increased your sensitivity to alcohol, you will need to continue to avoid over-drinking, especially on a regular basis. To remain sensitive to alcohol and get more for your money, you have to drink less often and not so much. We'll be telling you how to do that in the chapters ahead. But before that, let's consider how to evaluate drinking. The next chapter will help you decide if you, or someone you know, might be called a "successful" or a "problem" drinker.

6

Evaluating Your Drinking

Few people agree on how much is "too much." Some consume 15 drinks every day and never let their behavior get out of line. Yet others have one drink and they are already in trouble. It depends largely on who is deciding how much is too much.

While working with alcohol abusers in Germany a few years ago, we were told by one of the first patients we met that he didn't think he had a drinking problem because his consumption was "about the same as everyone else's." And how much was that, we asked. He replied that he started the day with a half-liter bottle of beer (a little more than a half quart) around ten in the morning, had another bottle or two with lunch, a bottle or two at midafternoon break, a couple with the fellows after work, another one at dinner, and then of course in the evening went out to a *Gasthaus* for a couple more just to socialize with friends and family. Only about four or five liters a day, huh? Yes . . . but of course on weekends he might drink a bit more. When we raised our eyebrows, he defended himself by saying no one thought he had a problem. His wife and kids loved him, his boss said he was a good worker, the village preacher thought he was a good man, and he got along fine with his neighbors. In short, he behaved perfectly well except that he drank a lot. In his eyes, it was not too much. Indeed, it did not seem to be a strong negative influence in his life.

In contrast, it is always easy to label someone an alcoholic when the individual has drunk so much that it has seriously interfered with

69

job, marriage, and physical health. This is what Alcoholics Anonymous calls the "bottomed-out" alcoholic—the person who has lost so much because of drinking that he or she may finally be motivated by desperation to do something about it. The most serious abusers, or alcoholics, in some cases may even have developed a degree of physical addiction so that one reason for their continuing to drink is to avoid withdrawal symptoms, i.e., physical illness should they stop drinking. The fact that such addiction may occasionally occur is no justification for regarding even this extreme form of alcohol abuse as a disease, since their addiction is a *consequence* of prior overdrinking, not a cause, and there is little evidence to suggest that they were physically different to begin with. But this is just one kind of drinker—the most serious abuser. The vast majority of unsuccessful drinkers are *not* like this. To one degree or another they may drink too much, but they would hardly be called alcoholic. The vast majority of unsuccessful drinkers—and there are *millions more of them* than there are alcoholics—are fairly happy and productive people. For them, overdrinking is a recurrent problem just as overeating and smoking cause problems for some people.

All habits come in varying degrees. Smokers often measure their habit by how many cigarettes or packs they smoke a day. Dieters count calories (particularly excessive calories). Drinkers can count drinks. The more they drink, the more of a drinking habit they have. As with smoking or overeating, abusiveness is a matter of *degree*. The idea of degree of a drinking problem has advantages over the all-or-none traditional approach, which says a drinker either is or is not an alcoholic (and one does not normally get tagged an alcoholic until things are pretty bad). This after-the-fact definition tends to stick with problem drinkers—it is assumed that they have *always been alcoholics and will always be alcoholics*, even if they stay dry for forty years! This logic is unfortunate because it does not give drinkers a chance to rationally judge their own drinking habits until the situation is so serious that change is very difficult. It makes much better sense for drinkers to be encouraged to evaluate their drinking at any time, see how it might be changing, and decide what to do about it early in the game when it is easier to change than it might be later.

What can actually be done to change drinking habits depends mainly on *how much* is consumed and the various *consequences* of drinking. We use this information for rating drinking habits as a matter of degree. Using our system, you will be able to find out whether you, or someone you know, is a "successful" drinker, or a "mild," "moderate," or "serious" abuser, and what can be done about it.

How much, how often, and *how long* someone drinks are important basic measures of the habit. The more people drink, the more frequently they do it, and the longer they stay at it when they drink, the greater the drinking habit. If they drink every day, but only two drinks, there may be no problem. If they drink once a month, but put down a dozen drinks when they do, they are more likely to have a problem. Furthermore, if a drinker typically rather quickly reaches a peak BA of 80 and comes right back down, the risk is not so great as it would be if he or she stayed at 50 for much of the day, as our Bavarian friend did. The reason is the total amount consumed. For example, a 150-pound person who drinks to a BA of 80 in an hour would have to consume about four 12-ounce beers, 5 ounces of hard liquor, or 16 ounces of 12 percent table wine. By comparison, the same person drinking from noon until 9 P.M. and maintaining a BA of 50 would consume twice as much alcohol (which the body must process). So the total amount consumed has to be considered as well as the peak BA, even though BA is more directly related to "intoxicated behavior." As a general rule, then, the less you drink, the shorter the time, and the lower the frequency of drinking occasions, the more moderate your drinking habit. The higher the BA, the longer it lasts, and the more often it occurs, the greater the habit.

But blood alcohol is not the only factor in alcohol use and abuse. No matter how much and how often a person drinks, the various *consequences* of drinking have to be carefully considered for a more complete picture. The most important consequences are *vocational, social, marital, economic, legal, physical, and personal.*

Drinking may affect *job performance.* Even without a bad hangover, workers are often less alert and skillful on the job because of drinking the previous night. Serious hangovers are just more obvious in their effects, sometimes keeping people from being able to work at all. Some abusers actually insist they don't have hangovers because, in reality, they always have one. Dean Martin once quipped that he feels sorry for people who don't drink because when they wake up in the morning, that's as good as they're going to feel all day. Maybe so, but could it be that a heavy drinker might no longer remember what it is like to be free of a hangover in the morning? Some drinkers simply don't know until they manage to stay dry for a few days. In our experience, if such individuals can manage to totally abstain for a few days, they feel much better and often are delighted about their productivity on the job.

Some drinkers also tend to drink when they *socialize*, and they socialize only with other people who drink, thus markedly restricting their lives. To the extent that they limit their friends to other drinkers and drink whenever they have contact with other people, their lives are socially confined by their drinking. When alcohol limits us in any way, socially or otherwise, we should take note. It is costing us something.

Alcohol can also cause *marital problems* because the drinker may be fine when sober, but change from Jekyll to Hyde when drinking. If there are problems they don't get settled when sober, they often become worse through drinking because emotions, including those involved in marital fighting, are usually exaggerated under the influence of alcohol. In addition, excessive alcohol can interfere not only with the relationship but also with good parenting. The trials of children being raised (and sometimes abused) by heavy-drinking parents are familiar to us all.

Another important consequence of drinking is *economic*. Liquor is expensive and a drinking habit can put considerable strain on the family budget. A hundred dollars or more a month is a common alcohol expense, especially for bar drinkers. And that doesn't include what it costs society (all of us) in terms of inflated health insurance, care for alcohol abusers, increased auto liability insurance, and other costs for personal injury and property damage. In addition, we should consider lost work and lowered efficiency, which affect business productivity and ultimately our national economy (the lighter-drinking Japanese are tough competitors!). It is estimated that alcohol abuse costs America $42 billion a year, including $864 million for treatment alone.

Legal problems resulting from drinking can be devastating. The drunken driver may spend a lifetime regretting what happened if an accident occurs, may suffer jail time, heavy fines, expensive attorney's fees, and increased insurance premiums, not to mention the humiliation of the experience. A two-day sentence or major restriction of driving privileges is now mandatory *even for first offenders* in California, and this movement toward stiff sentences is spreading throughout the country. A recent Supreme Court decision in California allows drunk drivers to be tried for murder if a fatality occurs. While drinking and driving is the biggest problem (see Chapter 16, "Gasahol"), public drunkenness, child and spouse abuse, assault, robbery, murder, and crimes of passion also often involve drinking. The legal process for these drinking offenders is a burden upon us all, not to mention the personal loss directly resulting from their behavior.

The potential negative *physical consequences* from drinking were discussed in Booze and the Body (Chapter 3). While successful drinking apparently is not harmful, frequent and excessive drinking eventually takes its physical toll. One difficulty here is that we often don't see these consequences for many years, so they may not affect our drinking much until it's too late and the damage is irreversible.

The *personal pain* for both the drinker and his or her loved ones can be enormous. We suffer when we witness those we care about hurting themselves by drinking. (Ways to approach such a drinker will be discussed in Chapter 8.) Of course, a drinker may suffer a special kind of personal and very private anguish. Drinkers often *know* drinking is a problem but have found no way of successfully dealing with it. They may resist going to AA or the family doctor for reasons discussed earlier (stigma, abstinence as the only cure, etc.). The result is that they live in silent, helpless pain.

In addition to the miscellaneous consequences of drinking de-

DRINKING SURVEY

Score: Answer each of the following as honestly as you can:

_____ Job:

Score 0 if the drinker goes to work with a hangover no more than 2 times per year; score 10 if the drinker has a hangover 3–10 times a year but doesn't miss work; score 20 if the drinker works with a hangover more than 10 times per year or misses work one or more full days because of drinking.

_____ Social:

Score 0 if the drinker socializes up to half the time with nondrinkers or light drinkers; score 10 if 50%–80% of socializing involves drinking with others; score 20 if more than 80% of socializing includes drinking with others.

_____ Marital:

Score 0 if drinking is never or is rarely a point of dispute in the drinker's marriage or intimate relationship. 10 if sometimes; or 20 if often.

_____ Economic:

Score 0 if no economic difference is felt; 10 if it makes some difference; or 20 if drinking makes a big dent in personal economics.

_____ Physical:

Score 0 if alcohol has had no negative effects on the drinker's health; score 10 if minor effects; 20 if major effects.

_____ Personal:

Score 0 if alcohol is not a problem and the drinker never worries about it; 10 if he or she worries occasionally; and 20 if the drinker worries a lot.

_____ Drunk Driving:

Score 40 points if the drinker has had a drunk driving conviction in the past 5 years; score 20 if arrested for drunk driving but not convicted.

_____ Overnight Care:

Score 40 points if the drinker has ever had overnight hospital care for a drinking problem.

_____ Tolerance:

Score 40 if the drinker feels little or nothing at a BA of 55.

_____ Recreation:

Score 40 if the drinker nearly always drinks during recreation or relaxation.

_____ 5-Year Problem:

Score 40 if the drinker believes he or she has had an alcohol problem for five or more years, even though not all the time.

_____ BA Score:

Enter the usual *peak* Blood Alcohol figure while the person is drinking (from tables at the end of the book).

_____ Total:

Add all the scores and compare the total with the ratings below:

Total Score	Type of Drinker
0–110	Successful
111–150	Mild Abuser
151–200	Moderate Abuser
200+	Serious Abuser

scribed above, there are five "special indicators" that almost always suggest a serious drinking problem. These can be thought of as *red flags* which signal trouble:

1. *Drunk driving conviction(s)*
2. Having received *overnight hospital care* for alcohol abuse
3. Having developed *tolerance for alcohol* (feeling little or nothing at a BA below 55)
4. Having *no recreational activities* other than those involving alcohol
5. Having had *five or more years* of drinking problems, even intermittently, in the drinker's own opinion

Presented on pages 74 and 75 is a *Drinking Survey* for estimating success or lack of success with alcohol. It takes into account the amount of alcohol consumed, the life consequences of drinking, and also the five special indicators of a serious alcohol problem. Try it out on yourself or someone you know well who drinks, keeping in mind that it provides only a rough estimate of the seriousness of drinking.

If you or the person you are rating is a successful drinker, congratulations. You or your friend will want to be sure to stay that way and maybe even cut down a bit for any of a number of personal reasons. Chapter 7, "Setting Limits and Preventing Problems," tells successful drinkers how to be even more successful and what to do to prevent themselves from ever developing a drinking problem.

If the person in question is not a successful drinker, then the important question is what to do about it. Mild and moderate abusers can use the guidelines in this book with great effectiveness to become successful drinkers. But if the person being rated scored as a serious abuser, he or she should consider quitting entirely. This may require a giant effort and perhaps professional help. Other possibilities include Alcoholics Anonymous or a hospital inpatient alcohol program, especially if the serious abuser needs round-the-clock care to dry out because he cannot stop drinking on his own.

Serious abusers who are unwilling at this point in their lives to try to quit can try cutting down. We don't recommend it, but they may insist on trying. However, before we can endorse *any* drinking by an unsuccessful drinker there are two very important matters to be dealt with. One is that anyone with a serious alcohol problem in the past who is not now drinking should never start drinking again. Such a person's chances for successful drinking are just too slim. The other consideration is that all unsuccessful drinkers should be examined by a physician and should tell the doctor that they are concerned about their drinking and want to know if they are physically O.K. to drink. If they have medical clearance to drink, then they can use the methods and guidelines of this book which involve drinking to learn successful drinking.

Honest drinking records are critically important for the serious abuser, as the drinker and his or her family are ultimately the big winners or losers. If their drinking does not decrease to successful levels in a month and stay there for another two months, it is very unlikely that the drinker will ever succeed. In our experience some serious abusers have been successful at reducing consumption to reasonable levels, but those who do are highly motivated and are not so severe in their abuse of alcohol. Even then, they must faithfully keep on recording their drinking so that any changes can easily be detected. If they begin losing control, they must quit drinking or they will have to settle for the grim life of an uncontrolled abuser, because moderation does not work for them and sooner or later that fact must be accepted.

If this sounds like typical gloom-and-doom talk about alcohol, remember that the serious abuser is in the minority of people who overdrink. The vast majority of people can use our guidelines to become and remain successful drinkers. The first step in being a successful drinker is setting appropriate limits. The next chapter describes how to do that and tells successful drinkers how to insure against ever becoming a problem drinker.

7

Setting Limits and Preventing Problems

What is a successful drinking limit? It's drinking for an hour or less to a blood alcohol level under 55 and experiencing only positive consequences. That's it. If you drink like this, you stay within successful drinking limits and can discover ways to make drinking even more enjoyable. For example, don't work or do anything that distracts you from the good feelings you experience when drinking. Finish any necessary tasks so that you can be relaxed and comfortable before you have your first drink. Drink only to enhance the good things in life, not to escape problems or drown your sorrows. Drink occasionally rather than every day so your body does not adapt to alcohol and tune you out of the pleasant effects at moderate BAs.

MARIA AND HER LIMIT

Maria, a divorced working mother of two pre-teenagers, was a mild abuser who drank to a BA of 70 almost every night. When she became aware of the extent of her excess she determined just how much she had to cut down. Maria typically drank about 5 ounces of 80-proof whiskey over a two-hour period. She determined from the BA/weight table for a 110-pound person that two drinks—i.e., 2½ ounces of 80-proof whiskey in an hour—would bring her to a BA of near 55. Instead of pouring herself a drink right away when she got home, Maria changed clothes and took the kids for a walk, often to a nearby park, before starting the evening chores. Sometimes she watched the news on TV or relaxed in a hot bath, but in any case she delayed her evening responsibilities and her drinking for at least half an hour. She also started shopping on weekends for the week's groceries, freeing time on weekdays and avoiding a last minute rush to the store. She moved dinner time up by half an hour, too. The effect was to shorten her total drinking time by about an hour. When Maria got around to having her first drink, she measured out 2½ ounces (two shots) and poured it all in a glass. Then she made herself a drink, using about half the liquor and put the rest in the refrigerator. She drank each of the drinks over a period of about 20 minutes. After the second drink, Maria's BA approached 50, stayed around 50 for about 15 minutes, and then began to decline. Dinner was served at this time. Maria also no longer drank every night. Sometimes it was easy for her not to drink and sometimes it took a conscious effort. But Maria wanted to avoid becoming more tolerant to the effects of alcohol and cheating herself out of the enjoyment she got from drinking to moderate BAs. In this manner she was able to benefit from the extra enhancement that drinking offered her on many evenings for relaxing and enjoying the company of her children without sacrificing her pleasure from drinking. She no longer experienced any of the negative effects of a BA over 55. Maria is an example of the type of person who can make an abrupt change in drinking habits without any trouble. All she needed was some basic information about setting limits and preventing problems.

Let's elaborate on what a successful drinking limit is and why. Staying under a BA of 55 is critical because above 55 the chance of problems increases greatly. All the bad consequences that *can* result from drinking are much more *likely* to happen. Even though the drinker may not realize it at the time, regular BAs over 55 will interfere with overall health and shorten the life-span. This is bad enough, but other negative outcomes such as being a bad parent or friend or lover, spending a lot of money, making poorly thought-out or quick decisions that are regretted later, causing a car accident, suffering from a hangover, acting like a fool socially are far more likely as the BA goes above 55. It is worth staying below 55 to minimize the possibility of these troubles as well as for health reasons.

Not drinking every day, even below 55, is also important. The daily drinker runs the risk of becoming tolerant to the effects of alcohol. Without knowing it, daily drinkers may be very gradually increasing the amount consumed because *more is needed just to get as high as they are used to getting*. This means that even successful drinkers should consider becoming more successful and insure against developing problems by eliminating any drinking that offers few benefits, such as at lunchtime or on evenings when they do something that drinking does not really enhance. Better yet, the successful drinker should target one day or more each week when there will be no drinking. This will disrupt the body's tendency to adapt and become tolerant to alcohol. Once a drinker becomes more sensitive to lower BA levels, he or she will get just as high as usual, but with less booze. This means getting *more* from drinking *less*.

The reason for drinking for less than an hour is to ensure all the benefits of a rising BA. Remember, *rising BAs feel good*. Falling ones don't feel as good and the drinker cannot keep the BA rising for more than an hour without running the risk of going well over 55. So by drinking to a peak BA of less than 55 and then stopping, it is possible to have *the good without the bad*. When the drinker stops drinking, it is desirable to do something else that is fun and thus reduce the desire for another drink. Eat, sleep, read, watch TV, or engage in other activities to end a drinking period. If the habit of "having a drink" is hard to break, have one—but make it a nonalcoholic drink. Stock up on your favorite nonalcoholic beverages for this purpose.

Special occasions or holidays may cause some drinkers to exceed the successful limit perhaps two or three times a year. But if they do it without risking their own or other people's welfare by driving or attempting other responsible actions, they can still regard themselves as successful drinkers. It could even be argued that under certain conditions occasional drinking above 55 is fairly successful.

SOL'S SEMI-SUCCESSFUL DRINKING

Sol loved his Saturday night poker game and wouldn't miss it for anything. He and his cronies had been doing it for over ten years and never once had there been the slightest problem related to his drinking. Sol was a good poker player and usually came out ahead. His social behavior was entirely appropriate and he never drove home after the game. Depending on whose house the game was played at, he made arrangements to be driven home by his wife, to be dropped off and take a taxi home, or to spend the night. Yet he routinely drank to a BA of 80 to 90 on these occasions.

When drinkers without significant personal problems occasionally or even regularly, such as once a week, drink to a BA above 55, behave acceptably, do not avoid problems, never drive or make important decisions that affect their own or others' welfare, we would consider their drinking to be excessive but fairly successful. Perhaps the only negative consequence they will experience is the long-run health effect. But if they know what they are doing, are willing to accept the health risk, will insure against problems, and have a demonstrated record of good behavior when they do it, then they are "semi-successful" drinkers.

In general, however, the simple rules described earlier for applying successful drinking limits will insure against problems. The already successful drinker will probably have little trouble using them, and the next section of this chapter on preventing problems will tell successful drinkers how to stay that way. But unsuccessful drinkers will need to invest more energy to take advantage of them. Although some unsuccessful drinkers can immediately start drinking within safe limits once they are aware of the specifics (as Maria did), it is probably easier for most unsuccessful drinkers to drink one or two drinks less for a week, and then one or two drinks less than that each week thereafter until consumption has declined to the successful limit. For most people, gradual changes are easier to live with than abrupt ones. Of course, good drinking records are essential to plotting your course.

Besides gradually decreasing the amount you drink, you can shorten the drinking time by starting a bit later or ending a little earlier, as Maria did. And you can measure out the drink limit in a separate container to make it easy to realize when the day's allotment is being approached and when it has been reached (which is harder to do when under the influence). Each week will mean pouring out a little less. You can keep away from people and places where you are likely to go over the limit. Cut out drinking during the times when it will be easiest, such as lunchtime or an evening when working late. Or plan an entertaining event to replace drinking on some particular evening when you would normally drink. Each of these strategies will be detailed in later chapters.

In the previous chapter we considered whether it is possible for *serious* abusers to become moderate. To answer this question, one of our research studies examined the ability of *currently drinking* serious abusers to learn moderation. This research, which took into account degree of abuse, showed that the *more serious* the abuser, the *less likely* the chance of success with controlled drinking. Our clinical experience has been that most serious abusers are better off not even trying to become moderate. It is actually easier for them to become abstinent. One major reason, as pointed out earlier, is that moderate BA levels don't give them what they want when they drink. Serious abusers are so tolerant to the effects at moderate BA levels that unless they can continue drinking to excess, they don't get high. They might as well not have started drinking in the first place. So the chances are they will drink to excess when they drink. Only a small percentage of serious abusers who are at the lower end of the serious abuser range and who are very highly motivated succeed at moderation. And they can't expect to stay that way without being on guard forever. Also, *drinkers who have been serious abusers but are not drinking currently should never attempt drinking again.* The risk is simply too great. Instead, they should try to make life as satisfying and happy as possible without the use of alcohol, a topic that is discussed in detail in Chapter 14, "Going Cold Turkey."

The strong, even compelling, desire of some serious abusers for more alcohol once they have started to drink, and their unpredictably succumbing to that desire by drinking to excess, is referred to as "loss of control" by some people. Such drinkers have a high tolerance for alcohol which requires that they drink to unsafe and unhealthy BA levels if they want to feel intoxicated. The evidence is slim that such drinking is caused by anything physical. There *is* evidence, though, that it is caused by what drinkers *expect* to happen when they start drinking alcohol ("one drink, then drunk"), as well as the consequences sought by drinking. One recent study even showed that drinkers given nonalcoholic cocktails craved more if they believed they were drinking alcohol. Regardless of cause, such "loss of control" drinking is a sign that abstinence is the best solution to a drinking problem.

For serious abusers who are currently drinking and feel strongly about attempting moderation, we recommend only one try. But first they should be *examined by their doctor and get medical clearance to drink.* Failure to become moderate from this one last effort means that abstinence is the only solution that will work. If they have tried and failed, then *their* limit is clearly no alcohol at all.

Preventing Alcohol Problems

The guidelines for setting limits can also be used by successful drinkers who want to prevent the development of a drinking problem. Establishing and using your own personal guidelines is like taking out an insurance policy against alcohol abuse. It takes very little effort and will actually *increase* your pleasure from drinking. We regard it as a golden opportunity which successful drinkers should not pass up. Here's how to establish guidelines for yourself to prevent a drinking problem:

Know your BA: Look at your weight and BA table at the end of the book. Note how many drinks someone your weight can have in an hour and remain at or below a BA of 55. The lower the BA you are satisfied with, the better, so never increase your drink limit because you are under the safe limit of 55 and have room to spare. For example, a 150-pound person could drink as many as 3 drinks in an hour. If you are satisfied with 2, though, you should drink no more than 2.

Drink for an hour or less: If you drink for much longer, you will either drink an unhealthful amount, even though your BA might stay under 55, or your peak BA will exceed 55, or both. The body adapts to the effects of alcohol in less than an hour so you will need a lot more alcohol to stay "high"—and that "high" will lose its pleasantness anyway as your BA exceeds 40–50. So plan carefully to drink for an hour or less to get the good effects without the bad. If you are going to be at a drinking function for several hours, plan at which hour you will do your drinking and drink nonalcoholic beverages before and after your drinking hour. It is often easy to delay the start of your drinking (and to benefit from watching others drink as suggested in Chapter 5). Doing it this way will give you the feelings you seek when you drink.

If you drink more than an hour, sip and substitute: If you don't mind not getting high (which might seem like a waste of drinking time to some drinkers), you *can* spread your drinking out over more time. You will still be drinking successfully if you drink no more than you would in an hour to remain below a BA of 55. For a 150-pound person, for example, this would mean the 3 drinks allowed in an hour would be spread out over the entire drinking period.

Realistically, however, we know that some drinkers may occasionally drink more than their successful limit at a lengthy drinking event. This doesn't mean you should cast caution to the wind and drink with abandon. There are still big advantages to setting some limits. *Even though you might drink an excessive amount, you can remain below a BA of 55*, which is very important because you will avoid many negative consequences. See your weight/BA table for the number of drinks someone your weight can consume over two, three, four, and five hours and remain below a BA of 55. Sip tall drinks or substitute nonalcoholic beverages in between alcoholic drinks. For example, if you weigh 180 pounds, during the first hour you can drink about 3 drinks and 1 drink per hour after that. Even though you drink a total amount that is unhealthy (seven drinks), at least you avoid a BA above 55. This is not entirely successful drinking, but it is *far* better than no limits at all because you will not be subjected to many unnecessary risks.

Measure your drinks: Use a normal shot glass (1¼ ounce) and not a king-sized one, so you can be sure of your BA.

Drink only to enhance an already good mood or occasion, and not to avoid problems or escape from stress: This book will help you deal with these problems without alcohol if you don't already know how (see especially Chapter 14). Alcohol should be reserved for making good things better. So pay attention to the good things that happen when you drink. Don't be distracted by responsibilities. Take care of them before you start drinking or plan to tackle them on another day.

Ideally, drink only occasionally rather than daily so you will avoid becoming tolerant to the effects you drink to achieve: Daily drinkers must be extra careful because of tolerance and must monitor their consumption often to be sure that the amount they drink isn't increasing. We recommend recording consumption for one week every six months. Keep the records in a file for comparison. If you detect an increase, stop drinking for a while to increase your body's sensitivity to the effects you want to experience when you drink. Reread this book and do those things necessary for a return to more successful drinking, such as using more alternatives, learning to relax, becoming more assertive, dealing more effectively with hot spots, or even seeking professional help for personal problems. Knowing when to do this is determined from your drinking records, which will show that your drinking is on the rise.

Never drink and drive: Make provision for transportation in advance of the event. Someone should agree to remain sober and do the driving. And never hesitate to call a cab or spend the night.

Be on guard about your drinking during periods of greater stress: You are better at solving problems if you drink less rather than more, although many people do just the opposite. So watch out during periods of extra stress and actively and consciously avoid increasing how much and how often you drink at these times. Again, reread this book when such periods arise in your life and you are concerned that your drinking might be affected.

The old saying "a stitch in time saves nine" certainly fits drinking. The amount of effort required to correct a developing drinking problem is much less than that required to overcome a long-term problem. So make it easy on yourself if you are an unsuccessful drinker and get a handle on your drinking as soon as you can. Prevention and early intervention are the best and easiest avenues to successful drinking.

We have described how drinking habits can range from successful to very unsuccessful. Sometimes concerned friends or relatives of a drinker can help. The next chapter, "Getting Support from Family and Friends," will provide suggestions for those who want to help someone who drinks.

8

Getting Support from Family and Friends

This chapter is addressed to the concerned others in a drinker's life, but the drinker too may benefit from the suggestions given here. An essential aspect of changing drinking habits is understanding the reality that *only the drinker can do it.* No one can stop a drinker from drinking (short of locking him or her up in jail). A drinker can always find a way to get a drink. Some drinkers are particularly skilled at finding excuses to drink. This means that, realistically, relatives and friends of a drinker are limited in their influence. We will help clarify what can and cannot be done and how to go about it.

What you as a concerned friend or relative can do depends largely on the drinker's willingness to let you help. If the drinker wants to change and desires assistance, you are in a good position and we will help you use it to best advantage. If the drinker has ignored the question about drinking and is touchy about it, you must be cautious. Taking responsibility for his (or her) drinking by "talking to him" about it is almost always a losing proposition. The drinker may not be ready to deal with it at all. In such cases, about the best a relative or friend can do is leave this book in a conspicuous place. You want him to start on his own if possible. There is a good chance the drinker will at least look through it because privately abusers usually are concerned, or at least curious about their drinking. If they do glance through this book, chances are the approach will seem to be less condemning and more acceptable than anything previously encountered. The drinker may even start working on the problem and you won't have to do much initiating at all. He might even be willing to talk about it with you, but don't push it. Realistically, at first you can expect only some slight interest and not much more.

Many drinkers may show no interest at all in talking about their drinking. Our experience is that problem drinkers often need time—even months—before they work up to doing something about their drinking. Dieters and smokers often do the same thing. Just because we should lose weight doesn't mean we are immediately going to start doing something about it. We often have to work up to the sacrifice, and that doesn't happen overnight. At some point, however, we must finally stop avoiding the problem and give it our attention. To do this usually means we have to see a way out—a way that we think might work for us. If we can picture just how we are going to do it, our chances of actually trying are much better. The trick for the friend or spouse is to lead the horse to water. The drinker's *attention without avoidance* is the first step toward change.

If a few days pass and the drinker shows no sign of reading the book, raise the issue. But do it at a good time—never when either of you is angry or upset. Pick a time when you are both sober and feeling good. Then be caring and direct about it. You will most likely make the drinker defensive if you simply start pointing out the bad things about his or her drinking. He already knows all that and will not want to be verbally beaten. If he does let you give him a hard time, he may just be "taking his punishment" for previous over-drinking episodes, which restores him in his own mind to good standing so he can get drunk again. Defensive drinkers also might counterattack with something bad about you, making the whole situation worse than if you hadn't mentioned their drinking in the first place. So start off saying some good things about them. Tell them they are good parents, do great at their work, have a fine sense of humor: mention any other personal qualities you admire. Think about it beforehand so you can be sincere. If it would not be too unusual, you could even say "I love you" or "you are a good friend," or some similar expression of caring. Whatever you say, make it positive and supportive. Then say you found this book interesting and different, with practical, down-to-earth suggestions for drinking less and enjoying it more, or for quitting. Give them time to react. You should not try to accomplish a lot at once. In fact, if you push them to say they will change, it might work against you. Our experience has made us skeptical when a drinker suddenly announces he or she is going to instantly cut down or stop drinking. They usually don't make it even though they express the greatest sincerity.

RICHARD THE SINCERE

Richard was like many other alcohol abusers who become highly motivated to do something about their drinking right after a serious incident. He had gotten into a fight with a good friend over a trivial matter (best car on the road). Since he could barely remember the incident the next day, his wife angrily gave him all the gory details. Richard was profoundly embarrassed and upset. He called his friend with a heartrending apology and promised his wife from the bottom of his heart that he would never touch another drop of liquor again. He seemed sincere and convincing about his intention to quit drinking. For two weeks he never touched a drop. But then one night, after a particularly good day at work, Richard stopped off at a bar with a few friends. He planned not to have anything to drink but before long found himself tipping just a beer or two—after all, beer *is* the drink of moderation, isn't it? He was shortly downing beers right along with the rest of them. After two hours Richard had consumed more than 10 beers and, as you might predict, returned home as drunk as ever to a very unhappy wife. Once again, he was remorseful and repentant the next day and, with all sincerity, decided that he must quit. (His wife was no longer as enthused about his chances. She was sincere too—in her doubt about Richard's likelihood of success.)

What is necessary for change, in addition to sincerity, is a more careful consideration of what actual steps are involved and how to go about taking them. No amount of sincerity will lead to change if we have no idea how to change. During your first discussion, if the drinker is at all agreeable about trying to change, consider yourself successful. That may be all you can do for the time being. If he wants to talk more about it, that's even better. This book should provide a basis for useful exploration of the topic. But whatever happens, don't badger, and try to end any discussion on a positive note.

One difficulty in helping a drinker is that concerned friends or family sometimes make more of the drinker's problem than is helpful. The drinker's behavior is taken personally and it is assumed by the concerned person that he or she has an important role in causing or maintaining it. Concerned others sometimes may interpret the drinking as designed to hurt them. They make life meaningful for themselves (but in a negative sense) by focusing on the drinker's abusive consumption as the main issue in *their* lives. Most abusers' drinking is not caused by or even highly related to the people closest to them (unless there are serious relationship problems). Concerned others will be more effective in helping the drinker and encouraging self-help if a more neutral and objective view of drinking is maintained.

The first six chapters of this book presented basic information about drinking, including an evaluation of the kind of drinker a person is. The first real do-something-about-it chapter is Chapter 9, "Motivating Yourself." Motivating means getting down to business by increasing the drinker's motivation to reduce consumption or quit drinking. If the drinker is ready to begin, you can offer your help as described above. If he (or she) doesn't want your help, or changes his mind about it at any time, back off. Make it clear that you are available—and caring—but will *not* take the lead, be responsible for him, or deal with his drinking problem in any way unless he asks you to. If you try to take on any responsibility for the drinker, you lower the chance of success in the long run. Patience. It took him a long time to get this way and he is not going to change overnight. It's a slow, gradual process and overeagerness can work against you.

How should the concerned helper respond to episodes of drinking? Avoid subtle punishments like looks of mild disgust or barbed questions such as "How are you this morning, dear?" Negative comments about their drinking will generally produce little more than sarcastic replies. Let drinkers suffer the consequences of their drinking *on their own*. If the drinkers have hangovers, do nothing special or nice. Ignore their distress, don't give them aspirin or special food. Do not wake them for work, either, unless you always have.

Try to express what you *feel*, not what you think or want. Use "I" statements rather than "you" statements. Express your *own* feelings and reactions to their drinking. Feelings are yours and cannot be disputed. "You" statements are often judgmental, evaluate the drinker's behavior, and cause defensiveness, rationalizations, and sometimes counterattacks which result in unpleasant arguments and fights. Instead of demanding "You should cut down on your drinking because you are so bad when you drink," try saying "I love you, but it's painful for me to be around you when you drink too much." Other examples of "I" statements expressing *your own* indisputable feelings are:

> "I don't feel comfortable around you when you have been drinking too much."
>
> "I worry about the repercussions of your drinking."
>
> "I am concerned about our relationship and the family's financial stability."
>
> "When you do not respond to my concerns, I feel hurt and not important to you."
>
> "I do not want to fight with you. It is your choice to drink, but I suffer from it and am worn down from living with it."

Children of alcohol abusers often feel guilty about a parent's drinking because they mistakenly think they are partly the cause of it. They do not need to accept such responsibility and accompanying guilt because they are almost never to blame. Sure, they have lived with the drinker and been a part of his or her life. But when people have children they accept the responsibility of raising them and there is nothing special about raising children that causes heavy drinking. Of course there are stresses in raising children, just as there are in many other aspects of living. But drinking is only one of many ways adults can react to stresses, problems, and responsibilities.

Many friends and relatives fall into a habit of giving special treatment to a person who drinks too much, allowing the drinker to play the role of "poor victim" who deserves special kindness. That kindness, of course, helps the drinker avoid the negative consequences of drinking and thus subtly encourages him or her to keep right on getting drunk. So stifle your natural helping instincts and let him grovel, groan, and feel terrible. Refuse to take responsibility for him; do not protect, comfort, or pamper. Instead, honestly but calmly say you are upset and ignore him as much as possible. Never let yourself be put in the defensive position of answering the question "How could you have let me do that?" He drank, not you; make it clear that you are not responsible for anyone's behavior except your own.

Often people close to a drinker are struck by the great remorse that is shown following a drinking episode. The travail is heartrending, the apologies sincere. He or she will earnestly plead with you to accept an apology—and thereby let him off the hook. Don't do it. Be businesslike, perfunctory, and unresponsive. Don't argue about it, and be prepared for anger when you do not accept an apology, but stick with it. You *are* upset and an apology does not magically set things right.

Sometimes a spouse will tolerate heavy drinking for years, then in desperation leave and initiate divorce proceedings. Sometimes, at this point, the behavior may change as the drinker belatedly takes seriously what is happening. But often by then it's too late. It is better to express your concern when the drinker can more easily change and make life better for both of you.

Try to focus on the positive things you can do. Pay special attention to your drinker when he or she is *not* drunk. Be attentive, pleasant, and reward sober behavior. Encourage expression of feelings and concerns while sober so drinking is not needed to be expressive or honest. The drinker will discover that you show little interest when he is drunk and irresponsible, but provide warmth and affection when he is sober and functioning well. The way to help a person become successful in daily life without alcohol is to systematically encourage success, nurture it, and help it grow.

9

Motivating Yourself

St. Augustine once said, "Lord, give me chastity—but not yet." If you are a drinker, that is exactly how you may feel about giving up drinking or cutting down. Many drinkers know they should change but aren't yet ready to do it.

There's a big difference between thinking you should change and putting your heart into making a change. How many times have you heard people say they *should* stop smoking, or they *should* lose weight? What they are saying is they know it would be good for them to live their lives differently. But knowing what is good for people rarely motivates them to change much. It would be good for all of us to quit eating junk food and get more exercise, too, but the chances of actually making a change, just because we know we should, are slim. People rarely change *unless they have an emotional reason to change.* We use expressions like "putting your heart into it" or "burning with desire" when we talk about strong motivation. To begin to make a change and to keep at it long enough to be successful requires an emotional commitment. Most of the suggestions for achieving motivation in this chapter are aimed at helping the drinker become emotionally aroused enough about his or her drinking to change it. And the drinker is the only one who can do it.

Our first suggestion is to use a simple and well-proven motivational technique: *Carefully record your drinking and your progress.* This strategy is similar to that used by dieters when they count calories and record daily weight. Success results in feeling good and making an even stronger commitment to controlling appetite and intake. We discussed techniques for keeping track of drinks in Chapter 5, "Drink Watching." Just one reminder here: record each drink *before the first sip*. This will sensitize you to how much you are drinking at the most crucial moment as well as provide accurate information on consumption. For maximum impact we recommend making a graph by putting days along the bottom and the number of drinks up the side, marking the daily level before going to bed. Post the graph in a suitable place, such as on the refrigerator or liquor cabinet door. You may think twice about taking that next beer when a chart right in front of you reflects your progress.

Next, *consider your reasons for changing drinking*. Many drinkers have well-rehearsed excuses to justify drinking at any time and any place. "I stopped off for a few with the boys after work because I had such a good day." Or, "I needed a few to drown my sorrows after a terrible day." Or, "I'm so happy I just want to celebrate—where's that bottle of champagne?" "I wish I weren't so depressed—maybe a drink or two will help." If a friend should call in the evening and suggest meeting at a bar for a few drinks, it's a sure thing an excuse can always be found, and the drinker never has to fairly evaluate the decision to drink. We suggest throwing out the old reasons for drinking and substituting a new list of reasons for drinking less. Both health and personal reasons can be used. A few examples:

> I will live longer.
> I am a great parent when sober.
> I become aggressive when my BA is over 55.
> I save $150 a month by not drinking.
> I feel like a whiz-kid on the job when I don't have a hangover.
> My friends like me better sober.
> My health will improve.
> I will get a promotion at work.
> I will kiss my beer-belly goodbye.
> Drinking less is dieting and I'll lose weight, look better, and feel healthier.
> Next year I can go to Hawaii on the money saved.

Written descriptions of the "drunken self" can be prepared and used in the same way. Ideally, the description should be written by the drinker. If the drinker would like help, it's O.K. for others to give it, though they should try to come up with something that embarrasses or provokes unpleasant feelings in the drinker.

A twenty-eight-year-old woman wrote the following description of her drunken self:

> When I get drunk I become loud and scream at my husband, which he doesn't deserve. I say things like:
> "You aren't very smart."
> "Can't you do anything right?"
> "I hate your mother and you're just like her."
> "I've slept with better men than you!"
> I tend to get aggressive and break things, even on purpose sometimes.
> I slap my kids in the face hard and will tell anyone to shut up.
> I drive dangerously, which frightens me to death when I think about it the next day.
> People don't like to be around me when I drink too much—they say I'm overbearing.
> I'm afraid to be close to people because my breath is so bad.
> I sometimes get sick in front of my family and friends.
> I feel absolutely horrible the next day.

You can use *snapshots of loved ones* with captions such as "Daddy, I love you" or "Please don't drink." Such photos can be posted in a private place such as a bedroom closet or carried in a purse or wallet, and provide powerful motivation to change drinking habits.

Drinkers will be more confident and secure about drinking successfully if they have a *written description of their limits.* Guidelines for limiting drinks can be written quite easily. Check the tables at the end of the book to see how many drinks a person with your weight can drink in an hour and remain below a BA of 55. Then write it out as shown in this illustration (for a 160-pound person):

1. I will drink for no longer than one hour.
2. I can drink up to 3 drinks during that hour.
3. If the drinking occasion is longer than an hour, I will have a nonalcoholic beverage between drinks and can have only one alcoholic drink during each succeeding hour.

Most drinkers in our experience don't really know what they look like or sound like after they have been drinking. And most are not pleased when they find out. *Seeing or hearing oneself intoxicated* for the first time can be a major boost to the desire for change.

The ideal way of giving people feedback about their behavior is on videotape, which unfortunately requires rather expensive equipment. In our treatment program we make videotapes of most clients as the first step in assuring their motivation to change. A sober look at a videotape of their drunken behavior graphically illustrates for the drinker the changes that occur, ultimately for the worse, as they go from sober to drunk. There is just no way to comfortably deny the slurred speech, loss of coordination, stupid stories, and unpleasant attitudes that often appear after too many drinks. Drinkers are normally not very aware of these changes, typically being convinced that when drinking they are clever, witty, and amusing, when they are actually boring, sloppy, and overbearing. Seeing themselves the way they really are can thoroughly rattle a drinker's cage. At that point, if given some clearcut guidelines for changing, such as those provided by this book, a drinker is more likely to get started. We have followed this procedure with hundreds of people and are convinced that graphic feedback of this sort is one of the best motivators for change. Since we are well aware that most of our readers will not have a home camera–video system, we suggest the use of simple photographs and sound tape recordings as a substitute. Most people do have a camera and a tape recorder, or can easily borrow or purchase them (some cassette tape recorders are quite inexpensive). Here's what to do:

If you are going to get drunk, someone responsible must remain sober to take pictures and make recordings as instructed below. That "helper" should be an individual who is supportive, positive, and caring. He or she must avoid passing judgment, telling you what's right and wrong, or giving negative feedback, as we've already discussed. All the necessary equipment should be available, including a card for recording consumption. The drinker should eat a light meal one or two hours before the session. (Too much food slows down absorption of the alcohol into the blood, which prolongs the session and makes it more difficult to get good pictures and recordings. If the drinker eats nothing at all, he may become intoxicated too fast to permit the helper to properly record the changes along the way.) Everyone present should have a good understanding of what's going to happen. The drinker must understand the purpose of the "drunk session" beforehand and agree to cooperate and not demand more drinks when the helper says it's over. The kids should be in bed or at a friend's home so no one else is around. The telephone and the door should not be answered. The helper should know what the drinker is like when he or she gets drunk and, if there are doubts about handling the situation, a second helper might be necessary. Strict attention must be paid to the task.

Record several speech samples and photograph the appearance of the drinker *before* drinking begins. One good way to do this is to develop a routine. Parts of the Field Sobriety Test, used by the police on suspected drunk drivers, work well. For example, have the drinker try each of the following while you record the spoken parts on tape and take photos (of course this can be done any time as a quick sobriety check):

A. Walk a straight line heel to toe.
B. Stand on one foot with head tilted back and arms outstretched.
C. Touch each finger rapidly to the thumb, one after the other, back and forth.
D. Write out the alphabet starting somewhere in the middle.
E. Hold one hand steady and clap the other against it, first on one side and then on the other, as fast as possible.

F. Turn around in a circle.
G. Tongue twisters: "Peter Piper picked a peck of pickled peppers," "She sells seashells at the seashore," "Black bugs' blood," or "Rubber baby buggy bumpers."
H. Count backwards from 100 by 7s (100, 93, 86, 79. . . , etc.) or even by 3s.

Once the testing routine is down pat, the helper should be alert during the drinking session to snap photos of anything bad that happens, like vomiting or sprawling out on the floor. Close-ups of drunken faces with spaced-out, emotional, or silly expressions often look grotesque in the cold light of sobriety. Two drinks between tests are about right for most people, but you may have to experiment. If the drinker is getting intoxicated too fast, slow him or her down and take the test more often. If he is drinking too slowly (perhaps on purpose to avoid looking bad), have him drink a bit faster. But wait long enough for the alcohol to be absorbed into the blood—usually 20–30 minutes after each drink.

Keep track of how much is drunk and be sure the drinker is protected from being hurt by stumbling and falling, or from breaking things. He must get high enough to show some of the effects so it may be necessary to arrange the environment to protect the drinker and also to protect the household goods. When enough pictures and recordings have been accumulated, provide no more drinks and instead feed the drinker, put him or her to bed or in front of the TV. They will have agreed in advance to let the helper control how much they drink, because the whole purpose of this exercise is to get useful photos and recordings—not to get drunk just for the sake of getting drunk.

The photos and recordings from the drinking session are to be used mainly to heighten motivation to control drinking. For those drinkers who are working toward moderation, the photos and recordings can also help during the early stages of a drinking period. Reviewing and posting photographs is important. The drinker should pick the ones that are *most emotionally upsetting* for pinning up or carrying in wallet or purse. Think of the places where the drinker is most likely to be tempted. For example, tape pictures on the refrigerator door, on the inside of the door to the liquor cabinet, in the car, or at work. (If company is coming or for any reason you don't want them posted, take them down and put them back up later.)

The drinker should listen in privacy to the recordings of speech changes from sober to drunk every other day for a week, then weekly thereafter.

The photos, recordings, lists, descriptions, and graphs we have just discussed are motivators that can be used effectively when the drinker is sober and before starting to drink. Those working toward moderation should also use them *while* drinking in order to maintain their motivation to stay within moderate limits.

Praise and encouragement from friends and relatives can be a positive outside source of motivation. As mentioned in the last chapter, those who cannot refrain from passing judgment about success or failure or telling the drinker what to do should not be involved. The best thing that concerned others can really use for positive effect is praise and rewards. When a drinker is trying to change, friends and relatives should avoid punishment or even subtle words of a negative sort—they can all be used as an angry excuse for going back to excessive drinking. Praise and reward for small changes—a smile, a touch, a hug, all can be helpful. People usually make changes gradually, and after two steps forward will make one backward. A good rule is to watch for improvements and reward them. Ignore setbacks. A statement like "You sure handled yourself well at the party last night," accompanied by a hug, goes miles farther toward success than a frown and "Did you make a fool of yourself yesterday!" A drinker must stabilize and consolidate at a new level of improvement and continue to get praise for a while (one to two weeks). Then further small improvements can be rewarded again.

Praise should be meaningful to the drinker and may need to be subtle. Some drinkers like a big obvious show of approval and others do not, or at least not in public. A helper should know the drinker and what he or she likes. Helpers can be creative in how they please the drinker for making an effort. Besides words, hugs, pats on the

back, and other encouragements, there are favorite foods, things he
or she likes to do but never gets a chance to do, such as enjoying entertainment, being alone, or being free from usual chores.

If the drinker seems to use alcohol in order to be more expressive
and emotional, then make it a point to give your attention and approval for self-expression, even a little of it, while sober. Motivation
to change will be heightened if use is made of the strategies presented in this chapter. Once highly motivated, a drinker has a much
better chance if the steps toward success are clear. The next chapter
will focus on dealing with "hot spots," situations in which drinkers
have trouble controlling their drinking.

10

Managing Hot Spots

Drinking records are the key to identifying hot spots, those situations in which you tend to overdrink. People, places, time of day, emotional state, purpose of drinking—each of these has something to do with how much you drink. You must know your hot spots so you can do something about them.

THE CASE OF PATRICK

Patrick was a mild alcohol abuser who kept records of his drinking for several weeks. Somewhat to his surprise, he discovered that one of his hot spots was social functions involving his wife's business friends. His wife was a professional woman who frequently asked him to join her for dinner with her associates. She also sometimes had dinner parties at their house and in both cases Patrick was expected to be fairly sober and good company to everyone. It was important to his wife that he stay reasonably sober and not cause any embarrassment. Unfortunately, Patrick noted from his drinking record, these occasions often resulted in his drinking *more* than usual and well above his successful limit. He found himself feeling rather anxious as the evening approached so he often had a drink or two before they went out or in advance of the guests' arrival. The guests were not really his friends, but the situation required that he be with them and make the best of things. So he tended to gulp 2 or 3 drinks rather quickly at the beginning and rapidly become somewhat intoxicated. His behavior was usually acceptable during the first hour or so, but once his BA got above 55 his social skills deteriorated along with any interest in being friendly. He might, for example, laughingly hold back a snack tray from an overweight guest, commenting, "You sure don't need any of these." The result was that his wife complained about his behavior on these occasions, although she did not specifically relate it to his drinking. But Patrick's drinking record clearly showed that his blood alcohol on these occasions was in the 80–90 range, while his more typical BA when drinking socially was 50–60. Thus, keeping track of how much he was drinking revealed that social events with his wife's business colleagues were a major hot spot, causing him to drink more than usual and to suffer some unpleasant consequences. Fortunately, Patrick and his wife were open and direct ("assertive") in speaking up about their views of the problem and were able to work out a solution. (Without being assertive, they probably would have been angry, aggressive, or resentful and never have achieved a good resolution. We will discuss assertion in the next chapter.) Patrick agreed to eliminate the drinking before these events, set his limit at the number of drinks that would bring him to no more than 55, and negotiated with his wife not to linger at dinners out (which she had a tendency to do). Also, Patrick would occasionally get a break and not be obligated to go.

In Patrick's situation it was essential that he and his wife be able to cooperate and work constructively toward a solution. Sometimes drinkers can do it themselves.

THE CASE OF MARLA

Marla was a thirty-four-year-old woman in her second marriage whose two pre-teenage daughters from her first marriage visited every other weekend. Marla's drinking record clearly showed that on the weekends they visited she began drinking earlier in the day and drank far more than usual. This naturally started her thinking about why she drank so much when they visited. She certainly was glad to see them and they usually had a good time. She loved them very much and paid a lot of attention to them. In fact, as she thought about it, she paid so much attention to them that she ignored her own needs. Marla realized that she enjoyed devoting herself to her kids but that she exercised no limit on it. The result was that she became fatigued and worn down from focusing exclusively on them and what they wanted to do. She would start drinking to compensate for these negative feelings, which seemed to help. At first it made things O.K. again but, because Marla still never really got to do what she wanted to do, or felt any weekend break from the stresses of her *own* daily life, she failed to stop drinking at a moderate level. Her parenting ability naturally declined and she wondered if her kids had noticed how intoxicated she was becoming. Of course, all this made her feel guilty and privately concerned about her drinking. But once Marla isolated this hot spot she was able to do something about it. She realized it was important for her to do some of the things that *she* wanted to do and not devote herself exclusively to the kids—for *their* sake as well as her own. Marla decided that the girls could do what she wanted to do, at least part of the time, whether that was swimming, playing cards, watching a TV show that she liked, cooking a dinner that she preferred, or going out to a movie or for dinner. Marla even allowed herself some time alone to read. It turned out that the kids were perfectly happy to join their mother in her fun or even to leave her alone for a while rather than unrealistically expecting her to do their thing all of the time. For her kids' welfare it was important that she take care of herself. Also, she became more serious about using guidelines for moderate drinking. She stuck to her drink limit and drank for a maximum of an hour and a half. These strategies together were successful in controlling this important hot spot for Marla.

RATING HOT SPOTS

Roughly speaking, you can rate hot spots in much the same fashion that you estimated the degree of your drinking habit in Chapter 6. A situation in which you drink to a blood alcohol level between 56 and 75 with minimal negative consequences is a mild hot spot, between 76 and 100 with a bit worse consequences is a moderate hot spot, and BAs in excess of 100 and with more serious consequences are serious hot spots. Of course, it is also important to know where you drink successfully. When your BA is consistently under 55 and only positive consequences result, you have identified a fairly safe place to drink.

WHAT TO DO ABOUT YOUR HOT SPOTS

For mild hot spots you need to be on guard and prepared with specific strategies to cope with your tendency to overindulge. Moderate hot spots require that you be very alert and possibly avoid those situations. Serious hot spots generally require that you avoid them altogether if possible.

Being on guard means that you know your drinking limit. You must estimate how long you are likely to be at a particular drinking function and how many drinks you can consume while remaining within the 55 limit. If necessary, plan to space drinks between non-alcoholic beverages in order to do so. During the hot situation, keep an accurate drinking record so you know your approximate BA at all times. If necessary, heighten your motivation for moderating your drinking by glancing at pictures of your drunken self, examining your list of reasons for controlling your drinking, or reading a vivid description of your drunken self, before the event begins (or even during the event). You may also want to rehearse your script for turning down drinks and shorten the total time you will be at the event. You don't have to be the first one there or the last one to leave. Using these guidelines conscientiously will help control most mild and many moderate hot spots. If not, then avoiding them altogether may be essential if you want to be a successful drinker.

THE CASE OF JANET

Janet was a businesswoman who frequently went to a cocktail lounge with a number of associates after work. Everyone was expected to drink and Janet was no exception. Unfortunately, she usually accepted the many drinks that were bought by others and felt obligated to buy a round in turn herself. The result was a routine blood alcohol of between 60 and 70 when she was with this congenial group. There was clearly no doubt about this when she kept a careful drinking record. Janet decided to assert herself and simply refuse drinks, but she found this to be most unpleasant. Not only did her colleagues put great pressure on her to drink, but Janet found that she actually couldn't enjoy being there unless she went along with the crowd. Drinks would pile up in front of her and she was chided for being a "party pooper." She tried leaving early, which helped some, but then she found that the whole situation was not very much fun anymore since everyone teased her about "bugging out." Janet gave up on that approach. Looking at the whole situation, Janet realized that she had rationalized joining them because it was "good for business." When she thought about it, though, they did very little business and a lot of joking and drinking. Her final decision was to avoid going at all. Janet soon learned that everything was better as a result. She missed her friends some now, but she went home sober, enjoyed her family more in the evening, and was better on the job the next day. Her associates eventually adjusted to her absence, stopped commenting on it and asking her to join them. Actually, they seemed to respect her more for doing what she thought best for herself and she got along as well as ever with them at work.

Janet's example shows that sometimes, when the hot spot is serious enough to defy a more moderate solution, avoiding it altogether works out best.

PLANNING THE DAY

Your hot spots might be anywhere—at home in the evening, in bars at lunchtime or after work, or at parties. Wherever they are, it is important that you know about them so that you can make plans to deal with them. Some people have a tendency to mix too many drinks while standing around where drinks are being served, such as a friend's kitchen. If so, when at that house you can make it a point to locate yourself in the living room. Sometimes a particular type of drink says "have another" because it goes down so easily. Plan to drink something else. We think it is better to *write out* your plans and guidelines. Then you can refer to them as often as necessary and you do not have to depend on your memory to know what to do. Whether you have a daily or a weekly hot spot or just an occasional one like parties, it is far better to have a clear, rehearsed plan of action. Describe the conditions as specifically as you can. Write down the time of day, the place, the people involved, your customary emotional state, and the reason for being there. See if you can't accomplish your purpose with an alternative (to be discussed in Chapter 12). If not, be on guard with specific strategies like shortening the drinking time, substituting nonalcoholic drinks, being assertive in refusing drinks, and so forth.

The next chapter, "Handling Pressures," may be helpful since it deals with being assertive in refusing drinks and, in a more general sense, the power of positive assertion in getting your daily needs met reasonably and to everyone's satisfaction.

11

Handling Pressures

One of the realistic problems in cutting back any habit, whether it be alcohol, cigarettes, or food, is that pressures from other people encourage overindulgence. When smokers light up, they offer you a cigarette out of courtesy. When a hostess serves a fattening dessert, she expects everyone to partake. When we pour ourselves a drink, we assume that others will follow suit and have one too. All are the result of social convention, the desire to please others and share the good things in life. Yet good intentions do not always have desirable results.

Perhaps the most valuable skill for a person trying to cut down on sweets, cigarettes, or alcohol is the ability to say no and make it stick. We have all encountered the extra push that greets our resistance:

"Have some of Liz's fantastic German chocolate cake. Let me give you a good slice."

"Sorry, I'd better not. I'm trying to lose weight."

"Hey, we're all trying to lose weight, but how often do you get a chance at homemade cake?"

"Well, it does look good, but I've really got to cut back."

"Come on pal. Liz put in hours of hard work to make this especially for you. You can at least have a little so she won't feel bad."

"Well, OK., just a small piece."

"Relax, you're going to love this cake. It's sensational."

So a big hunk of boundless calories finds its way to our plate, stomach, and waistline.

If you stand your ground and resist further, you may get angry reactions like these:

"Hey, what is this? You think you're going to be Mr. Slim or something?"

"I've seen you inhale food like a vacuum cleaner. One piece of cake isn't going to make any difference after twenty years of pigging-out."

"Come on, the only time we get these special desserts is when company comes. If you don't eat, we won't get them anymore."

The variations centered upon taking a drink express the same insistence and demands that we drink despite an expressed desire not to:

"Come on, have another one. This is your buddy you're drinking with."

"One more drink isn't going to hurt you. You know how to put it away, I've seen you do it plenty of times."

"Hey, this is a party! I'm going to freshen that drink for you. No arguments about it!"

Being pressured in the name of friendship to indulge in something we are resisting for health reasons is an odd contradiction. In effect, the "friend" is violating our right to make our own choices, but doing it with good intentions. Yet, by definition, friends are people who do *not* violate our rights. This is perhaps why we often give in to friendly arm-twisting, because to resist and stand up for our right to say no might question the person's motives and friendship. Yet giving in to such pressure in any area of life leaves us open to manipulation by others. If they can make us feel guilty, ashamed, inadequate, weak, or a "spoiler" of other people's fun, then we will be more likely to give in and do what we honestly do not wish to do. Whenever this happens, *our* rights are being violated. Why? Because it is our right and nobody else's to decide what to eat, drink, and smoke, what to do or not do with our time, our body, and our property. Does any one of us believe that others should make those choices for us? Of course not.

The core problem, then, is to stand up for the right to make our own choices, and this inevitably requires some hassle, especially if you are a person with a history of *not* making your own decisions. You will have to speak out, say what is on your mind, and doggedly refuse to do what you consider undesirable. You must protect your inalienable right to make your own choices. We are talking about *being assertive*, an important requirement for successful living in today's pressure-filled society. People who are nonassertive, who let others habitually bully them into giving up the right to make their own choices, usually are not happy. They feel like victims, pawns being used, taken advantage of, and manipulated. They might say, "How did I end up working on this project? I didn't want to do this." Or perhaps, "Here I am having another drink. Why can't I say no and make it stick?" Or, "Well, I'd better go along with Fred and do what he says. I don't want a hassle about it, but there goes my weekend!" Have you ever thought to yourself, "I can't imagine why I bought this stuff. How did that salesperson get me to agree to it? Damn, what a pushover I am!" This is, in fact, a correct assessment because the nonassertive person *is* the classical "pushover" or "doormat." An individual who considers himself or herself to be a "nice person" or "helpful type," but in reality just cannot say no, will never feel really happy because of an inevitable lifestyle of being used and abused.

Not everybody, of course, can be pushed around. Whenever there is somebody being pushed, there is a pusher. It is important to stress that we are *not* suggesting pushing others around as an alternative to being pushed yourself. Pushers are usually *aggressive* people who violate others' rights, take advantage, and manipulate. The general public often confuses being assertive with being aggressive. Aggressive people are those who demand what they want, and it's just too bad for anybody whose rights stand in their way. Sadly enough, although they may indeed get some of what they want, aggressive people are rarely happy with themselves either, since they naturally get little positive feedback or human warmth from others. Aggressive types are often avoided and tend to generate hostility and counter-aggression when they dish it out. Being assertive and standing up for your own rights does *not* mean taking advantage of others. It merely means being honest and open in expressing your desires, not letting others make choices for you, not making choices for them, and being willing to compromise with others who will meet you halfway.

When it comes to drinking, being assertive means making *all* your own decisions about whether, when, and how much you drink, and standing up for your absolute right to make those choices despite what anyone else desires. (Along with the right to make choices, the assertive person recognizes the *responsibility* for making sensible life choices, including those related to drinking—in the last analysis, we cannot push any responsibility for our drinking behavior onto anyone else.)

The practical problem in becoming assertive is that once you have decided to make your own choices, you have to get that message across to others, and that's not always easy because they may not want to hear it. You may know your decision about alcohol but, unless you convey it assertively to others who want you to drink, the decision is of little use. Being assertive and getting the message across to others in any area of life requires some basic behavioral and verbal skills. These skills can be learned if they are not a part of your present style. They are nothing surprising. Think for a moment of the saddest pushover or most easily manipulated "milktoast" you know. Imagine he had something he wanted to talk to you about, perhaps concerning a disagreement. How might he tell you? Picture him walking into the room. He shuffles around, probably looking at the floor, hands clasped in front, glancing away nervously if you catch his eye. He may smile in a sick sort of way as he informs you he is upset. He mumbles, hesitates, stammers, and lets you know with every facet of his behavior that you can walk all over him, insist he was wrong, and finally make him feel bad for even bringing the question up. He may actually end up giving you an embarrassed apology for mentioning the problem. We have all known someone like that, the extremely passive and nonassertive person, and we all know how he is treated by others: like a doormat. What is most instructive about these people is that their behavior nicely illustrates to some degree a lack in all the basic skills required to be assertive. We hope you are not entirely like the man in our extreme example. But most of us could improve somewhat. So let's look at the basic behavior needed to be assertive. If you already have assertive skills, fine— and congratulations. That puts you one step ahead. If you don't have them, or want to improve, then practice and get them. There is nothing magic about learning new social skills. They require motivation, self-observation, and practice.

BASIC ASSERTIVE BEHAVIORS

The important elements missing from our classical pushover's performance are: (1) eye contact, (2) audible speech, (3) fluency, (4) appropriate emotion, (5) body language.

Eye contact: We all know about the "eye games" that are played in our society (some of them have special significance between men and women). When one person looks away, he or she acknowledges dominance by the other. Those who cannot look you in the eye in a confrontation have lost half the impact of their message. If you have something important to tell someone, you *must* look them in the eye! If it makes you uncomfortable to do that, then look them in the nose or look them in the eyebrow. They can't tell the difference! You don't believe it? Have a friend look at different parts of your face while you try to tell exactly where their eyes are fixated. The farther away they are, the larger an area of your face they can look at while seeming to be looking you in the eye. From six feet away they can look at your chin or ears. Across the room they can look you in the chest. To you, it seems like eye contact.

Audible speech: Next, speak up, make your voice loud enough to be clearly heard. If someone at a party says to you, "Here, let me fill your glass," and you mumble, "Oh, uh, no thanks . . . uh, I think I'll just . . . well . . . stick with this. . . ," what do you suppose their response will be? "Come on, get that glass up here! That's the way." (Blub, blub, you've got a new glassful.) You have to speak up clearly. Try one of these:

> "No, thank you, I have enough for now."
> "I appreciate the great service, but I don't need any more right now."
> "No, no." (Big smile, hand held over the glass.)
> "I'm cutting down and have plenty right here."

Fluency: The person pushing drinks must hear your words spoken fluently and without hesitation, indecision, or a tone of "Come on, convince me to have one more." Stammering, lots of "uhs," gaps, and mumbling all reduce the impact of what you say. Try listening to yourself on tape for one minute attempting to "sell something" to a friend. Describe all the good things about your watch, car, dog, whatever, and see how fluent it sounds. Then do it again, cut the gaps, speak up, speed up, be fluent. Check your performance. Do it again. In this manner you can quickly improve fluency and the impact of what you say. Then practice assertively refusing drinks in the same way.

Appropriate emotion: If you wish to be assertive, you should also show appropriate emotion when you are expressing feelings. Imagine someone is really pressuring you.

> "Hey, I am determined to cut down on my drinking and it's upsetting to be pushed to drink. Give me a break, huh?"

If you were upset enough to say that, you should *look* serious, not apologetic, confused, or amused.

Body language: Finally, learn to move your body appropriately. If you stand or sit in a position of submission with shoulders hunched, hands folded, and eyes on the floor, you will be treated as if no one heard or believed what you said about not wanting another drink. *Look the person in the eye, speak up fluently, sit or stand up straight, lean toward the person, and use expressive facial and bodily cues to help put across your message.*

HINTS ON PRACTICING ASSERTIVE BEHAVIORAL SKILLS

These simple assertive behavioral skills can be practiced by anyone at home. Have someone count the seconds of eye contact as you tell them something of interest to you (for three minutes). Then do it again and increase the time of eye contact until you are looking at them almost the entire period (not that you want to have a deadly fish-eyed stare, but keep high eye contact to show interest). To increase your fluency and volume, rehearse something you would like to say to a boss or friend or relative, getting it on tape. Listen to it and try it again and again. Get the volume up to clear levels. Overdo it at first, almost yelling, then you can cut back to normal. Get rid of the "uh's," silences, stammers, and stutters. Imagine you are practicing for a movie role. Once you have your lines down solid, work on expression by practicing in front of a mirror *silently* while exaggerating your emotions. Pretend you are acting in a silent movie. Try to get across your emotions with just facial expressions. Then put in body language—move your arms, hands, torso, head. Get excited!

Finally, combine the whole package and practice a few times with a friend, preferably an assertive person who can role play and help you to imitate. Have that individual give you feedback about what you did right and what could be improved. Social skills are learned by rehearsal. So rehearse.

THE VERBAL ASSERTIVE SKILLS*

Once you are able to look people in the eye, speak up fluently, and show appropriate emotion and body movements, you can more effectively use some assertive verbal tools. The most valuable verbal strategy in dealing with pressure is *repetition*. Many people will not hear what we are saying the first time we say it. In fact, they may not hear it until we have said it 10 times. So try being like a "broken record," clearly repeating your decision over and over until it finally sinks in. When a religious crusader or salesperson appears with a pitch at your front door, what do you do? Listen politely as they take up your valuable time? Or perhaps become angry, telling them off, slamming the door, or . . . do you remain calm, behave assertively, play "broken record"?

> "Sorry, I'm not interested." (Said with a smile, looking directly in the eyes, standing full height, leaning toward them.)
> "But I'm sure you will find much of interest in our new publication."
> "Sorry, I'm just not interested."
> "I'm sure your children would like it. How old might they be?"
> "Sorry, I'm not interested."
> "Won't you even tell me if you have children?"
> "Sorry, I'm really not interested."
> "Can't you say anything but 'I'm not interested'?"
> "No, because I'm just not interested."
> "I guess you're a lost cause."
> "That's right, because I'm really not interested" (closing the door with a smile).

* For a detailed description of verbal assertive skills, see Manuel Smith, *When I Say No I Feel Guilty* (New York: Dial Press, 1975).

Next time someone appears uninvited at your door, consider it an opportunity to practice assertive skills, and try playing broken record. You have no obligation to be interested, answer any questions, or accept the pitch. When dealing with questions of assertiveness, always keep in mind the question of rights: Is it their right to come to your door with a product or message? Yes, it is (unless your community has an ordinance prohibiting solicitation). But next, is it *your* right to refuse to answer questions about your family and not accept their product? Of course it is. Nobody is having their rights violated, and nobody has to get angry if you behave assertively. Try it.

Now, how can you tie this in with drinking? When a hostess says "Have another drink?" she may not really be asking a question. When you say "No, thanks," that message fails to register. So, no matter what she says, *just repeat it.* "No, I'd rather not." "I'll pass." "I definitely have plenty." "No, not now, maybe later."

Another useful verbal assertive skill is "fogging," making yourself into a sort of fogbank that is not affected by verbal barbs. People often try to get us to do what they want by challenging, needling, or irritating us. Once we become angry or upset, we often end up being manipulated by our desire to "show them."

> "Come on, Pete, have a drink."
> "No, I've been drinking too much and am cutting back."
> "Really? What's the matter, can't handle booze any more? Getting soft in your old age? Hey, this is not the Pete I know!"

The temptation, of course, is to say, "Listen, pal, I can handle whatever I want to handle and still drink you under the table!" It is a natural response to a challenge (particularly for men). But through the use of fogging we do not have to rise to any challenge, or even be irritated when somebody needles us. Here's how: Imagine yourself to be a fogbank and somebody throws a brick at you. What would happen? It would simply disappear into the fog. What if someone tries

sticking a few jabs with a needle into your fogbank? They get no response and no satisfaction. To become an instant fogbank, look for
the grain of truth in whatever is being said about you and, instead of
fighting back, simply agree with it. If you were Pete, you could try
one of these:

> "Yeah, maybe you're right. I'm not the old Pete you
> used to know."
> "True enough, I can't seem to handle it like I used to."
> "No doubt about it, I am getting older and softer."

If your drinking buddy tells you, "Come on, if you're a friend, you
won't let me drink alone," you might fog him with:

> "I suppose I could be a better friend, but I'm not going
> to have a drink."
> "I know you don't like to drink alone, but I don't want a
> drink at the moment. Let's sit and talk anyway."
> "You may be right, but I'll have a diet soda and no
> booze."

Your buddy may by now be somewhat frustrated by your changed
behavior (we often don't like it when people behave in new or unexpected ways—especially "doormats").

> "Hey, I never thought I'd see the day you would turn
> soft. That goody-goody act is disgusting!"

No need to rise to the challenge. Just fog him:

> "I never thought I'd see the day either, but here it is!"
> "I probably sound goody-goody and may disgust you,
> but I still don't want a drink."
> "Yeah, well, it's not easy being a goody-goody, but I like
> it. No booze for me."

"Well, I don't want to upset you, but I'm not drinking."
(Notice that whenever you fog, you also replay the "no drink for me" broken record.)

Often it is possible to reduce the pressure by offering a simple compromise:

"Just because I don't want a drink doesn't mean you can't have one. I'll have a soft drink with you."
"Even though I don't want a drink, that doesn't mean I don't want to talk with you. Let's take a walk and shoot the breeze."
"I still enjoy your company even if I'm not drinking. Let's go have some lunch. I'll buy."

We will not pretend that you can glibly sidestep all of life's pressures and interpersonal friction by simply responding with the right "line." What we are saying is that you can make your own decisions, calmly spell them out to others, and maintain your right to choose without having to argue or defend yourself. You *can* tell people that you honestly don't care about something important to them, that you have no good reason for preferring to do what you have chosen, that you are indeed illogical at times, but that in all cases it nevertheless is up to *you* to decide. You owe nobody an explanation or any sort of justification for your choices. Of course, you must grant the same rights to others.

People who have problems with drinking sometimes have a need to be assertive that goes beyond simply dealing with friendly pressures to consume more alcohol. Their drinking may, in part, stem from a basic inability to get their needs met. If you cannot get other people to provide what you need for day-to-day living, you can always get drunk. And sometimes you find that people treat you better when you are drunk, that you get "permission" to act out at center stage, be noisy, aggressive, let out your frustrations and pent-up resentments. All will be excused later because you "were drunk." We have all known the overbearing drunk, the person who with each drink becomes more and more talkative, dominant, pushy, and maybe even assaultive. Usually they are people whose daily lives are *somehow lacking.* The authors had a high school classmate who was famous for punching people in the mouth whenever he put away a few beers. Yet when sober he was a meek and rather timid person, somewhat lacking in social skills and graces. When drunk, he could express the frustrations hidden behind his normally passive smile.

Sometimes drinkers find themselves boxed into situations where drinking is expected and encouraged. The main character in *Days of Wine and Roses,* an advertising executive, was assigned a particular client because they both liked to drink. Drinking became part of his job, yet when they drank themselves into serious difficulties they both ended up fired from their jobs. Even a boss sometimes has to be told no, since no long-term career success can be based upon a cocktail-hour foundation.

We maintain that the proper use of assertive skills in daily life can help avoid this type of difficulty with alcohol. A person is unlikely to rely upon alcohol if he or she is able to stand up, refuse to be manipulated, abused, or pushed around. Such people can calmly say "No," or "I don't have time for that," or "I would like for us to spend more time together," or "We've got to talk, this arrangement is not going well for me." Assertive people do not have to be intoxicated to be expressive, honest, and openly go after what they want in daily life. They need not give in to pressure to drink if they prefer not to drink, nor do they have to consume alcohol in order to be comfortable in social interactions.

In this chapter we have been talking primarily to drinkers about how to make and carry out choices. But there is a clear message in this for the friend or relative of the drinker: Help that person learn to be better at self-expression *when sober. Listen attentively* when he (or she) is *not* drunk, before he demands your attention by ranting and raving. Encourage him to speak up, to be honest, to be expressive. Give him feedback encouraging assertive and expressive behavior. Think of yourself as helping to nurture and shape a new type of behavior much as you might work to nourish a fragile plant or newborn animal. Do not give permission to be out of control when drinking. If drinkers do get out of control, simply ignore, do not respond, and avoid them if possible. And remember that it takes time for a person to change. We have all had a lifetime leading us to where we are now—and we cannot change overnight. But you can help a drinker to self-help by encouraging responsible choices, expression of feelings, and standing up for his rights. An assertive lifestyle is ultimately of benefit to the individual and to everybody with whom that person interacts.

12

Establishing Alternatives

When a drinker cuts down on drinking, that means increasing something else to fill the time, preferably something that will turn out to be rewarding enough to compete with drinking.

Drinking does different things for different people. People drink in order to socialize, and to be able to play. Shifting gears from the responsibilities and high energy level of the day to a slower and easier evening mood is a very common purpose of drinking. The cocktail hour is supposed to serve that function. Some drinkers stop in bars for the cocktail hour to slow down their day, and others wait until they get home.

WINDING DOWN

Jack knew the crowd in his favorite bar very well. They stopped in every day after work during "happy hour" and most of them drank heavily. Jack felt he deserved a little pleasure after a hard day's work, so he typically indulged freely and came home with a BA of around 70. His serious, conscientious workaday attitude changed almost immediately on entering the bar. Even before his blood alcohol started to rise he was feeling good. His cronies told jokes, laughed it up, and complained about the usual problems of the day. Jack knew that his wife wanted him home in the evenings but she grew to accept his arrival around 6:00 P.M. rather than immediately after getting off work at 4:30. At least he came home, and usually with a smile on his face. On those rare occasions when he arrived sober, he was often grouchy and irritable. Jack told his wife that he needed a transition period before coming home and she felt that an hour or so in a bar was a reasonable compromise. When he did get home, though, Jack actually had very little contact with his family even though he was "with" them for the entire evening. He usually made another drink on arrival, said a brief hello to his kids and wife, and sat down to read the newspaper or watch the six o'clock news on TV. The kids might interrupt him with something about school that day, but he made short shrift of it to get back to his passive activities and drinking. Dinner was served and then he went back to the TV, but usually with no more drinking.

Jack was a very hard worker and pushed himself to produce. Alcohol helped him feel less guilty about being nonproductive after work. He also had the notion that he was a "family man," and told people so. In his opinion, just being with his family in the evening and on most weekends justified that. But the quality of time spent with them was actually very poor, as he avoided contact by tuning out or minimizing any interaction. He usually drank so much that he just didn't have the energy to solve any problems, play with them, or pay much attention to their needs. Jack had long ago decided it was his wife's responsibility to take care of the kids, so he wouldn't have to be so involved.

Jack is fairly typical of someone who uses alcohol to shift gears to a more relaxed evening mood. The easiest, most available and socially acceptable way he knew of to settle himself down from a hard day's work was to drink. Jack never even thought about an alternative that might do as well as drinking, although at times he suspected that he drank too much. And he would deny that he was avoiding his family since he was convinced in his own mind that he was a "family man."

In searching for alternatives to drinking, we are not suggesting that alcohol be eliminated from drinkers' lives unless they are serious abusers who must become abstinent. Drinking can be one of the things you do to enjoy life, but as they say, variety is the spice of life. Like anything else, drinking can get pretty boring if done routinely. And for daily drinkers, developing tolerance is a particular danger since they will gradually need more alcohol in the future just to feel as good as they do from their present drinking.

There are two psychological principles that explain why any particular drinking occasion is *more fun* if you don't drink very often. One, as mentioned above, is tolerance, which reduces your sensitivity to moderate BA levels. The other is deprivation, which means that if you don't have something you like for a while, it is usually better when you get it. If you haven't eaten all day long and a delicious meal is set before you, you will enjoy it more than if you have been snacking and are not very hungry. Together, tolerance and deprivation make drinking much more enjoyable if you do it only occasionally, as a special enjoyment rather than as a routine activity. In accepting this fact, you must be able to choose from other activities or events besides drinking that can accomplish the same result (such as relaxation, winding down, or diverting attention from work).

Overall, we think that life is experienced as more enjoyable and satisfying if people regularly engage in active as well as passive ways of making themselves feel better. Certainly, successful drinking is easier to achieve and maintain if you do. We do not argue that "natural highs" are better than any other kind. But we believe that adding alternatives to the ways in which drinkers satisfy their need for a pleasurable change in mood will enhance the quality of their lives, *including* the pleasure they get from drinking when they do it.

We think most people do not take advantage of many of the good things in life that are readily available to them. Most of us have engaged in activities in the past, but stopped doing so for one reason or another. We moved, changed jobs, graduated from school, developed new friends, or experienced other changes that altered the way we took care of our needs for emotional relief and pleasure. Alcohol can become a most competitive choice because of its ready availability, low cost, speed in accomplishing a change in mood, and general endorsement and encouragement from others. In contrast, seeking emotional change in a nonpassive way takes some active output of energy and effort. And many of us are not willing to make that effort. So we tend to get into comfortable ruts and then deviate very little from our routine, which quite often results in an overreliance on alcohol.

Our culture's work ethic and discouragement of active forms of play are partly responsible for excessive drinking. We feel guilty if we are not working, and drinking helps us overcome our guilt. As if an overdose of the work ethic weren't bad enough, the very pursuit of play, recreation, or "kicking back" is somehow not right either. Some people even regard it as immature or selfish to pursue individual pleasures. The person who goes to a movie alone is sometimes considered odd, since we are not supposed to have solitary fun. "Hedonism" has a sinful ring to it for many.

How does this affect people like Jack? They are overworked, anxious people who feel guilty about indulging themselves with a break from it all. Instead of an hour's worth of tennis, visiting a friend, or playing a musical instrument, they resort to the passive, and sometimes destructive, activity of drinking. Besides being approved—if not encouraged—by society, drinking gives them at least a temporary break from the pressures of everyday life. It's so much *easier* to drink than do something that takes a little planning and effort. The result is that many drinkers overdo it, become half drunk, and then have no energy to interact much with anyone.

We think that society often discourages healthy forms of letting go, while at the same time approves or even encourages the use of alcohol to accomplish the same purpose. For example, we frown upon teenagers who, after a hard day at school, "freak out" listening to rock music. We disapprove their dancing around the room with ecstatic looks on their faces. They should be doing their homework (something *productive*) or at least get out of our hair. Yet theirs is a genuine, nondrug high that helps them shift gears after sitting at a school desk all day long. Rather than discourage it, we should learn from it and imitate it. Active, exuberant, youthful play is one of the best and healthiest ways to wind down after a day of responsibilities.

We believe that if Jack were to find some satisfying alternatives to his hour in the bar after work, his life would improve a great deal. We agree that Jack needs something to help him come down from a hard day's work. And drinking *could* be a part of it. But if he were to do something else that he liked for that same hour he now spends in the bar—especially something physical—he could come home to his family feeling much more like indulging them with his attention. And he would probably drink less and enjoy it more. If he saw to it that his own needs for pleasure and relaxation were being met, but in another way besides drinking, he would feel better about himself and more like doing things with others. He might even enjoy playing with his kids, and he and his wife might go out together more often. After his day's work Jack literally needs "permission" to indulge his desire for a pleasurable break, to do something of his own choosing which engrosses and refreshes him. To encourage drinkers to find such alternatives is what this chapter is about.

REASONS FOR DRINKING

What purposes or functions *does* drinking have? There are several common ones and some that are unique to the individual. Some of the common ones are:

    Winding down
    Relaxing
    Socializing (enjoyment of others)
    Filling in the time (something to do)
    Playing or recreating (especially in the emotional sense)
    Changing your emotional or mental state

The last reason for drinking really includes or overlaps all the others. Psychologists talk about "altered states of consciousness," which is probably the common denominator of what the drug alcohol does for all drinkers to one degree or another. Drinkers usually "feel better" or at least less bad after a drink or two. They don't want to feel the same as they have been feeling. And alcohol is probably the easiest way to cause an emotional change. It is available everywhere, is relatively cheap, and works fast.

Finding out what else drinking does for the drinker will make it easier to come up with alternatives that do about the same thing. For example, alcohol may make it easier to enjoy others or approach the opposite sex. Drinking might be a cue or signal for being off work, for not being responsible. It's O.K. to play if you are drinking, or to drink if you are playing (the relationship between drinking and playing is repeatedly impressed on our minds by advertising). Drinking may indicate that it is time to relax.

Let's use the example of relaxation as the reason for drinking. Successful drinkers and nondrinkers have other cues besides drinking that signal emotional relief and let them know that the workday or responsibilities are over and they can relax. Turning on the radio, putting on jogging shoes, or getting into different clothes have the same effect as mixing a drink for many successful drinkers and nondrinkers. For less successful drinkers a couple of stiff drinks allow them to exit from their emotional world for a little while. In the short run, the outcomes are similar—relaxation results. But in the long run, if drinking is relied on too often for relaxation, then trouble is likely to occur. As mentioned before, one becomes tolerant to the effects of alcohol and needs more booze to get relaxed. Your health, your job, your financial and marital situations may all get worse and maybe even legal troubles will result from an overreliance on alcohol to relax. And you may be missing out on some of the good things in life besides drinking that are available to you.

We suggest that you study the common reasons why people drink, listed above, and try to come up with the purposes drinking serves for you. Write down your reasons and examine them at different times until you are pretty sure they are accurate before making your final list. Keep these reasons for drinking in mind as you look for alternatives.

SELECTING ALTERNATIVES TO DRINKING

The next task is to find activities or events that could substitute for drinking. Effective alternatives have to be pretty powerful to compete successfully with drinking. They should go beyond simply filling in the gap left by not drinking or reduced drinking, and compete with drinking by being truly compelling and satisfying in and of themselves. They can be almost anything from sports to meditation. Various experiences besides drinking are capable of changing one's emotional state. Listening to music, swimming, walking, working out at tennis, or anything else physical (including sex), a beautiful sunset or sunrise, reading a good story, meditation, video games, or simply being alone for a while are among the ways one can change one's mood for the better. The best way to find substitutes for drinking is to make a list of possibilities just as you might a grocery list—record items as they occur to you. You might think of something as you glance through a magazine, watch TV, or have a conversation. Carry the list around with you and add to it whenever you get an idea. Sometimes sitting down and thinking about what has been satisfying to you in the past results in good possibilities, as does reflecting on your dreams, fantasies, and daydreams. It may take several days or even weeks to come up with a good list. Once you have at least a dozen items, then rank them for *desirability*. Put your favorites at the top of the list, going on down to your less-favored ones at the bottom. Next, rate them for *availability*. Those items that are near the top of both lists are good candidates for becoming regular alternatives to drinking. Highly desirable items that are not readily available to you—such as a trip to Hawaii—might be rewards to work toward if you are successful for a significant period of time, but for day-to-day living you are better off with the more readily available alternatives. We usually need help today and cannot delay gratification of emotional needs for very long.

If some of your highly desirable and available alternatives serve the same function as alcohol, they are most likely the best ones to use. For example, if you now drink to shift gears to a more relaxed evening mood, but once enjoyed reading mystery stories to do it, try them again. You might have to go to a library, city park, or coffee shop to be able to read. But get some mystery stories and see if reading is fun and relaxing as it used to be. If so, start doing it routinely again. You will probably need more than one alternative. Some drinkers like to have several to choose from like items on a menu. Other people use the same one for a long time and then switch to another. You will have to decide what works best for you.

SCOTT'S ALTERNATIVES

Scott is a twenty-eight-year-old rancher who was concerned with his increasing tendency during the winter months to do little except sit around playing cards, and drink. He took out a pencil and pad, let his memory have free rein, and was able to list a number of things he used to do and enjoy. He then ranked them in order of desirability and estimated their availability.

Activity	Availability
Softball (Scott had loved it in school)	Local leagues in summer only
Guitar	Readily available
Astronomy (still has large home-built telescope)	Available on clear nights
Photography (could be combined with astronomy)	Readily available
Weight-lifting, body-building	Readily available
Stamp collecting	Readily available
Motorcycle trail riding	No longer has motorcycle; could get one and go on weekends
Attend stage plays	Occasionally available
Scenic camping	Occasionally available in season
Fly fishing	Occasionally available in season
Woodworking	Readily available (has tools)

After his list was completed, it was apparent to Scott that there were a number of activities quite readily available to him even during the winter if he would just make a minimal effort to get back into them. He could play guitar, lift weights, work on his stamp collection, and do woodworking at almost any time. Other activities, like astronomy and photography, were available often and could easily stimulate his interest. Some of his past activities, like camping, were obviously not available on a year-round basis but could be programmed into his life and perhaps used as "special rewards" for doing better with his drinking. He posted his list and made a rule that before taking a drink or going to the card room he would look over the list and try to direct his interest toward one of the other activities.

PROGRAMMING ALTERNATIVES INTO YOUR DAY

Your "hot spots" (Chapter 10) are a guide to when you most need an alternative. An alternative, or set of alternatives, that can regularly substitute for your hot spots will make a big difference in whether or not you drink successfully. If you know your hot spots and your reasons for drinking, and you have a good list of alternatives that meet the same needs drinking does, then you can begin experimenting. If your choice of alternatives is not working well, try something else. Perhaps you can talk it over with a friend or spouse. Find an enthusiastic partner if what you want to do can involve one. Feel good about experimenting with things that are fun. It is important for everyone's sake that you give yourself permission to enjoy. Everyone will benefit from a more contented, and sober, you.

One of the most common reasons why people drink is to relax. The next chapter, "Getting Mellow Without Alcohol," teaches relaxation as a voluntary skill.

13

Getting Mellow Without Alcohol

The desire to relax is natural enough. The question is how to get that way. Nearly every culture studied by anthropologists uses some chemical or psychological approach to the mellowing of mood, whether smoking hashish, meditating, practicing yoga, or the most popular of them all—drinking alcohol. Humanity has known for a long time that the various products of fermentation are capable of producing warm, pleasant feelings of relaxation. We human beings never seem to tire of this change in our state of consciousness. And the need is perhaps greater than ever before in today's high-pressure world. The issue in this chapter is how to do it and still be a successful drinker.

FOUR-MARTINI JILL

Jill was a high-strung woman who made no bones about drinking to relax and then some. She prided herself on making great martinis and prepared them with a flourish in a large shaker. She would gulp down the first one in about three minutes and pour another which she drank within ten more minutes. The effect of such rapid consumption was like taking a sedative—she calmed down fast. The change in her face, especially her eyes, was obvious to others—from tightened facial muscles, furrowed brow, and penetrating stares to slackened jaw and droopy eyes in less than fifteen minutes. That's what she wanted, as she admitted without reluctance. She rationalized her rapid drinking as necessary just to "get the first layer of civilization off." The next two, which she drank over an hour's time, served a different purpose in Jill's mind—"to get a little drunk." To others, her four-martini condition seemed to tune her out of everything rather than make her happy. Drug-induced relief from her very unpleasant state of tension resulted from the first two martinis, and the next two produced a wiped-out state of total escape.

The moral to the story of Four-Martini Jill is probably obvious. If Jill could somehow be already relaxed when she started drinking, she would drink less and enjoy it more. She wouldn't need the first two martinis to become relaxed. Starting to drink when she was already in a neutral or slightly positive emotional and physical state would make it possible for her to derive only the positive enhancements from one or two drinks in an hour's time.

Imagine you are sitting down following a tough eight hours at work, tending some wild kids, or wherever your hard days happen to occur. You think to yourself, "I feel wound up like a coiled spring. I could use a drink to relax." Taking a drink (or two or three) will indeed probably help relieve tension, but notice that instead of having a drink to feel pleasant and mellow, you would be taking a drink with the primary purpose of reducing negative feelings. Such drinking is not for enjoyment, but for relief. This is an important distinction, since drinking for relief from tension or stress is the use of alcohol for self-medication, not for enjoyment. In a sense, it is a waste of the benefits of alcohol, a "tuning out" rather than a "tuning in." We pose the question: If there were other effective methods available for relaxing, for getting rid of stress, for becoming mellow, wouldn't alcohol be more appropriately saved for enhancing the good things in one's life? We believe so, and will suggest some ways to relax and to get mellow that do not involve booze. When you come home from a bad day and can eliminate tension and stress without having a drink, then you can also be free to consider the various alternatives for your evening's entertainment, and having a drink remains just one possibility to consider, perhaps being passed up in favor of an alternative.

Besides, whether you drink or not, stresses will always exist. If you drink every time your life seems to be stressful, you may have to be drinking constantly ... and being tuned out by alcohol may mean that you avoid dealing with the stress-producing situation. In the long run that can only mean more stress, and more need to escape— a vicious circle.

PROGRESSIVE RELAXATION

For nearly twenty-five years psychologists have been suggesting that people learn "deep-muscle relaxation," a simple progressive method of identifying bodily tension and learning to turn it off. The beauty of relaxation training is that, once mastered, it can be used anywhere and any time. You can relax while waiting in the doctor's office, before seeing the boss, while talking to your in-laws, when stuck in traffic—anywhere! When relaxed, you are in no way impaired in ability or reactions as is the case when alcohol or drugs are used. There are only positive benefits from learning to relax your body voluntarily.

Some readers will be saying at this point, "But I know how to relax, that's nothing new." The fact is, you probably do *not* know how to relax, truly profoundly relax in a way that releases tension from your body. That's because you have never been taught how to do it and it does not come naturally. Still skeptical? Try something that may be helpful: Get yourself as relaxed as you can in your present situation. Tell your muscles to let go as much as possible (but don't fall out of your chair). Now, take an imaginary tour of your body, starting with your toes and working upward. Check for any tight or tense muscles. Look through your body carefully and you will find some unnecessarily tightened muscles. How about stomach muscles? Are they tense? What about your forehead? Is it furrowed and tight? Are your neck muscles relaxed? Are your shoulders hunched up a bit, your back being held rigidly in one position? Now concentrate your attention carefully for a few seconds on your jaw. Are the muscles at this moment relaxed or tight? Are you a jaw-clencher or tooth-grinder? (Sometimes dentists tell their patients that they grind their teeth while asleep—even when sleeping we may not really have the muscles of our body relaxed.) Many people spend their day with jaw muscles tightly clenched and are completely unaware of it. By evening, such muscle tension can produce a stiff neck, a dull headache, or a tired, aching jaw. Right now, while reading this, purposely clamp your jaw tightly closed and notice the feelings in your temples, at the base of your skull, up the side of your jaw and across the ridge of your teeth deep inside your skull. Inspect that tension carefully. Not pleasant, is it? Now slowly release that tension, telling those muscles to become increasingly flaccid and relaxed, and feel the tension slowly flow out and away. Concentrate for a while on how different those muscles feel when loose, as compared to when they were tight and tense. Now go beyond that. Try to relax those jaw and facial muscles even more. Concentrate on each muscle and command it to loosen, loosen more, and yet even more. The contrast should be extreme between your newly relaxed and comfortable muscles and the unpleasant experience of tension while your jaw was clamped tightly shut.

By progressively working through the entire body in exactly this manner, part by part, tightening and then loosening muscles, you can learn to sense tension in any part of your body and to command the muscles to relax. Doing this leads to a profound level of relaxation, so that you feel as if you are floating, warm and content, after just a few minutes of relaxation. The relief from tension through this kind of relaxation is such that it equals or exceeds the relaxation that comes from belting down drinks. And, once you are calm and relaxed, if you still desire a drink, you can then enjoy it for its enhancing pleasant effects and not squander it unnecessarily on getting rid of tension.

At the end of this chapter we will give you specific step-by-step instruction on how to learn to relax. Anybody can do it. Learning to relax is as simple as learning to ride a bicycle, and takes about as much time and effort. Once it is learned, like bike riding, it can be used wherever needed and will not be forgotten. And although a few half-hour sessions are required to learn deep-muscle relaxation, once the skill is mastered you can bypass the step-by-step tightening and loosening and go quickly to a profoundly relaxed state with a minimum of effort. This can include situations where only a few muscles need be used and all the others can be relaxed (e.g., driving or having a conversation).

Four-Martini Jill could obviously have used deep-muscle relaxation to great advantage. In just a few minutes she could rid herself of most lingering workaday tension. And she could do this at any time during the day to *maintain* a relaxed disposition and prevent the buildup that so often resulted in the self-administration of a big dose of alcohol after work.

Being able to let go and relax is an important ability for nearly everyone. Relaxing after work serves as a time of shifting gears, getting into that other part of life, the nonwork, fun-loving part that is a healthy aspect of a well-functioning person. As discussed in the last chapter, many drinkers fall into the habit of using alcohol to shift gears at the end of the day just because it is so easy to do. But a little extra planning could make relaxation just as convenient. Perhaps you can arrange time alone during the day for your exercises, or linger after work when everyone is gone so you can relax instead of stopping at a bar. Or drive to a private spot or scenic vista and do a bit of relaxation. Schedule time at home. A family will accept your need to unwind for fifteen minutes alone in your room after you get home. You can be straightforward and tell them exactly why you need that time. Besides, this is a good example for kids of ways to successfully reduce stress without resorting to drugs. Some people like to do a few minutes of exercise, like running in place or situps, before they relax. Remember, we all have a right to our own time, and nobody is so needed that he or she cannot insist upon a few minutes alone to help preserve mental and physical health. So insist, if need be, and do not feel the slightest impulse to apologize.

In addition to relaxation, we should also consider other nondrug methods of "getting mellow." How about listening to music? Sit in front of the stereo, turn on your favorite sounds, and just lose yourself. Hot tubs are superb for relaxing (as well as relieving pain in tired bones and joints). Or look out the window, enjoy a sunset, take time to smell a flower, jog, ride a bike, work a puzzle, do anything that will take your mind off daily troubles and you will find that your body automatically relaxes and lets go of tension. If you always sit down in an easy chair with a drink as soon as you get home, try doing the same thing with a diet soda and you will discover that even without alcohol you still become relaxed. Just sitting comfortably away from a stressful environment, sprawled in an easy chair, and forgetting about work, leads to relief of stress. The alcohol in the evening cocktail does not alone account for the shift in mood. There are many things going on around you that tell you it is time to relax and even *cause* your emotions to change automatically. Situations, people, and places that have been associated with letting go and relaxing in your past tend to acquire the power to relax you by themselves. This is called "classical" or "Pavlovian" conditioning and works automatically without any voluntary effort from you, other than exposing yourself to these things. Your favorite chair for relaxing, a room, a glass, a certain kind of music, a particular person, the newspaper, the time of day, all the things that have preceded or accompanied your becoming relaxed in the past, have considerable power to cause it by themselves *without* alcohol.

As we discussed in the chapter "Establishing Alternatives," there are many things to do besides drink, and this is also true when drinking has been used for relief of tension or stress. So go ahead, get mellow, relax, tune out of your troubles—there are many ways without alcohol.

STEPS IN LEARNING TO RELAX

We suggest that you purchase a commercial relaxation tape* or put the following script onto a tape so you can play it during training sessions. An alternative is to have someone you trust who is close to you serve as "guide" and speak these instructions during the training sessions. Either way, the voice should be low, slow, calm, and soothing in tone, leaving long silences with plenty of time between specific instructions for carrying them out. Practice where you will not be disturbed, with the phone off the hook, perhaps a "Do Not Disturb" sign posted on the door if necessary. No matter how busy you are, your business, family, or friends will survive without you for a few half-hour sessions over a period of days. Do these exercises with the help of the tape until they are so well rehearsed that the tape is no longer necessary. Each practice period will make it easier and faster for you to reach a profound, floating, super-relaxed state. But you must give sufficient time and effort if you expect results. Find the time and invest the effort—the results are well worth it.

Follow the instructions below. If you are really able to relax and to let your muscles soften and tension vanish, you may feel the almost mystical pleasant floating sensation that meditators have enjoyed for centuries. In addition, you will find that your mental image of the beach scene described at the end of the tape may take you to a near-dreamlike state in which you can almost hear the ocean, feel the sun touching your face, smell the flowers and sea air, and experience those warm emotions that go with meeting someone we hold very special. The purpose of practicing "visual imagery" is to demonstrate that you can mentally go beyond the ordinary and experience strongly pleasant sensations and feelings, all without alcohol. The power of relaxation and concentration can carry us far beyond what most of us allow in our nose-to-the-grindstone daily existence. And it is free, readily available, and good for mind and body. Relaxation is

* A good example is *Learning Relaxation*, available for $10.00 from: Center for Behavior Change, 1968 North Garey Avenue, Pomona, CA 91767.

helpful for blood-pressure problems, for getting over phobias, for worriers, and for just ordinary, normal folks who want to relieve stress and feel good each day. It is yours to use however and whenever you need it.

Tape Instructions

Record the following script on tape for relaxation training:

NARRATOR SAYS: *Settle into a very comfortable position, either on a bed, sofa, or in a recliner chair. Stretch out, be sure your body is supported evenly and you have room to move. Close your eyes and tune out the world around you, focusing all attention on your body. Slowly explore your legs, torso, arms, face, and head for any tight muscles, relaxing them as much as possible (Narrator: Pause for 30 seconds).*

Take a slow, deep breath, concentrating on the air coming into your body and then slowly flowing out. Do that a few times, focusing more and more, until your entire attention is on nothing but breathing. Take your time, feel and hear and experience your breathing (pause for 30 seconds). The world fades away as breathing becomes everything. Take a few slow deep breaths now and enjoy the tingling produced by the extra oxygen (pause).

Now, keeping your eyes closed, stretch your arms far out in front of you, imagining you are holding back a big weight. It is pressing toward you and you are keeping it back. Stretch your arms, hands, and fingers way out. Tighten those muscles as you push back the weight. Now concentrate on the feelings of tension in your arms, wrists, across the backs of your hands. Focus on it for 30 seconds or so (pause). Now let your arms drop and slowly let the tension flow out, down your arms and out your fingertips. Feel the difference as the muscles become softer. Let your arms settle to a relaxed position and command the muscles to soften even more, until they are completely, profoundly relaxed. Now compare the difference, enjoy the warm comfortable feeling of relaxation and contrast it with the ten-

sion and stress of a minute ago. Settle back and take a few slow, deep breaths (pause). Now repeat the weight sequence (long pause). Good!

Next, make both hands into fists. Tighten them until your fingers are jammed into your palms, the knuckles and thumbs stretched hard. Concentrate first on one hand and then the other. Feel the strain across the backs of your hands, in the wrists and fingers. Feel that tension intensely so you can remember it (pause). Now, slowly relax those hands, let them rest quietly at your sides and let the tension drift out and away. Again, notice the contrast in feelings, soft and relaxed versus hard and tense. Concentrate and try to relax them even more, beyond what seems like "completely relaxed" (pause). Again, repeat the sequence (long pause).

Next, scrunch up your shoulders as if trying to cover your ears with them. Tighten your neck muscles at the same time. Feel the strain across your back, over the shoulder blades, up the sides and back of your neck. Concentrate for a minute on that tension (pause). Command those muscles to slowly relax, letting your shoulders sink to a quiet and resting position, searching for any remaining tight muscles. Relax totally, feeling how different those soft muscles feel (pause). Enjoy the contrast, focus on the good feelings of relaxation, and try to relax even more (long pause). Repeat the sequence (long pause).

Now shift attention to your face and jaw. Scrunch up your face in a wrinkled mask, as if you had just tasted the world's sourest pickle. Mash your eyes closed and clench your jaw. Now slowly explore your face and notice the many tight muscles and uncomfortable spots. Feel the pressure around your eyes, mouth, cheeks, and temples. Feel the jaw pressure inside your skull, spreading around the back of your head. Check your scalp and you will discover that the skin is tight even there (pause). Now slowly let your face return to normal, the lines disappearing, the tight muscles getting softer and softer, until you can search all over and find no tension whatsoever. Relax even more, concentrate on eliminating every iota of tension, then notice how different it feels (pause). Compare the new, warm, com-

fortable face with the tense and tight one of a minute ago. Enjoy that comfort (long pause). Now repeat that sequence (long pause).

Next, tighten up your stomach muscles and chest muscles. Imagine that someone is about to punch your stomach and you are tightening to withstand the blow. The whole front of your torso will be rock-hard, protective, and tense. Notice those tight muscles, the taut feeling, the pulling and stretching (pause). Now that you have engrossed yourself in that feeling of tension, begin commanding those muscles to relax, to soften, and observe carefully while the tension melts away. Feel it go, replaced by comfort, warmth, softness (pause). Repeat the sequence (long pause).

Now move attention to your back. Lift yourself slightly off the bed or chair, using back muscles, straightening your spine and holding it that way. Feel the strain along your back, spreading around to your sides and up as high as your neck. Focus on that tension thoroughly (pause). Now slowly let it flow away, down through your body and out your toes (pause). Let warm comfort flow in, replacing that tension. Soak up that warmth, just let yourself be enveloped in relaxation as you command those muscles to soften beyond anything ever experienced before. Relax them even more (pause). Even more (pause). Fine. Now repeat the sequence (long pause).

Next, curl up your toes and at the same time tighten your leg muscles as if you were lifting a 300-pound barbell. Imagine you are the record weight lifter in your class and are now holding up a great weight. Feel that tension through your legs, ankles, and into your feet (pause). Let that tension stand out as you concentrate on it alone, noticing every area of discomfort as you hold that great weight (pause). After that discomfort is clear in your mind, tell the discomfort to begin leaving your body as the muscles relax, grow quiet and at ease. Let everything go and feel the tension flow out (pause). Compare the new feelings with those of a second ago. Relax the muscles even more, to total relaxation. Lose yourself in the comfort of relaxation (long pause). Repeat the sequence (long pause).

At this point you have covered some of the major muscles of the body. Now carry out a careful search of your body from head to toe, *looking for any other tense muscles. Tighten and then relax them (long pause). If you have a known problem area of tension that was missed in our exercise, such as tight biceps, neck, stomach, pinched lips, or thrusting tongue, take a minute to work on getting that body part relaxed as we have been doing (long pause). Good.*

Finally, let your eyes remain closed and feel the sensation of your whole body being relaxed, more deeply and slowly than usual. Take big, slow, deep breaths, leisurely inhaling and exhaling. Let each exhale represent a sigh of relief. Enjoy the good feelings of total relaxation (long pause). Now, eyes still closed, imagine yourself walking down a beautiful path near the ocean. Picture a curving trail between the trees, the sound of the waves ahead of you. It is May, the sun is warm as it touches your face, and the smell of the ocean rises over the fragrance of the trees and wildflowers. You step out of the forested area and the ocean stretches its turquoise beauty before you, the white sand glistening in the midday sunshine. It is a wonderful spot, nobody else is in sight, and you feel the sand between your toes as you walk toward the water, smelling the salt fragrance. You look down the beach, searching for that special person you know will be there to meet you. It could be somebody real or your imagined ideal person. You see each other, wave, and begin to hurry toward an embrace. This is someone very special to you, you smile, and your heart fills with warmth as you come close. It is such a beautiful day and you feel it is just great to be alive. Spend a few minutes vividly imagining that scene (long pause). Now that your body is totally relaxed, try to keep these feelings as you go about the rest of the day. Whenever you feel stress, find a place to sit back, relax, close your eyes, and get back into this comfortable state. It is yours to use whenever you like . . .

(End of tape)

14

Going Cold Turkey

This chapter addresses the question of how to quit drinking and enjoy life sober. Most serious abusers would rather become moderate than stop drinking completely. Alcohol is so important in their lives that to imagine living without it is almost impossible. Yet most sources of help insist that they stop drinking, and that's a major reason why so many serious abusers avoid dealing with their drinking problem. Unfortunately, some serious abusers wait so long to do anything about their drinking that moderation truly becomes nearly impossible. Society is partly at fault because moderation training is not available (certainly some serious abusers could have become successful drinkers if they had been helped at a time when their drinking was only mildly abusive).

Occasionally, the heavy drinking of serious abusers takes such a terrible toll that they stop drinking on their own. For heavy drinkers who are comfortable with their philosophy and methods, Alcoholics Anonymous has been of help. Professional therapy and specialized programs have worked for others.

Nearly all trained professionals recommend abstinence as the best solution for serious abusers, and so do we. Our research, and that of others, clearly shows that in the long run abstinence is more likely to work for long-term serious abusers. But our studies also show that not all serious abusers are alike. Remember, we measure abuse as a matter of degree and not as an after-the-fact, all-or-none, alcoholic vs. nonalcoholic determination. A small percentage of serious abusers can learn to be moderate and stay that way. Those who succeed, however, *are usually not so far along* in their abuse of alcohol as are most serious abusers.

In Chapter 6, "Evaluating Your Drinking," we showed how to determine whether someone is a successful or an unsuccessful drinker. We divided unsuccessful drinkers into three groups—mild, moderate, and serious abusers. We did not divide serious abusers into subgroups because we believe that for *any* serious abuser quitting is the best choice. His or her chances of success are better with complete abstinence. Yet we are practical enough to know that many serious abusers will never even try to quit. Some of them deny that they have a problem with alcohol. Others are not yet convinced that they have to stop drinking, so they still hold out hope of controlling it. Because research shows that a small percentage of them can become moderate, we have to accept it. And just as we are objective in evaluating the evidence on such a controversial issue, let us point out that drinkers *must* be totally honest in evaluating their drinking if they want to become successful drinkers or learn to enjoy life without alcohol. If the drinker is truthful and candid in assessing his or her drinking and comes out *just over the line* as a serious abuser (between 200 and 250 on the Drinking Survey in Chapter 6), he or she might stand a chance at moderation. For those well over 250, the chances are very slim. But if the drinker feels strongly about trying to become a controlled, social drinker before being willing to give up booze completely, then the chance should be offered.

By no means should you drink at all if you are currently *not* drinking and have had a problem with alcohol in the past. But, if you *are* presently drinking heavily and have been drinking abusively for a long time, one more effort at moderation is not likely to hurt. First, you should get medical clearance to drink and then you can use this book to try to learn moderate drinking. You might even succeed if you really give it your very best effort. But if you fail, the attempt may be important in setting the stage for accepting complete sobriety as a necessity. Abusers often feel that they should at least have had the chance to become successful drinkers before they can totally commit themselves to abstinence. We recommend a one-month attempt at moderation but with one *big* consequence for failure: If you don't make it at moderation within one month's time, and stay that way consistently for two more months, you agree with yourself beforehand to *quit drinking* completely. Try cutting down, using the guidelines and strategies of this book, and see if you reach successful levels of drinking and stay there. You will know if it's going to last by keeping careful, honest drinking records. If you never make it to the successful drinking level, or if your drinking slowly creeps back up to unsuccessful levels, then you'll have to go cold turkey. Going cold turkey may concern the serious abusers who anticipate "withdrawal symptoms" or feelings of illness should they stop drinking. However, unless you are a very serious daily abuser you are not highly likely to experience much physical discomfort. But should you have any doubts and would like some reassurance, consult a physician who commonly treats alcohol problems and get a recommendation as to whether or not overnight care is necessary for you.

This chapter will suggest how to stop drinking and stay that way by learning to enjoy life without alcohol. Eva is an example of someone who did.

EVA AND THE EMPTY NEST

Eva is a forty-eight-year-old woman who sipped wine most of the day. She had worked for six years after finishing high school and then got married, quit her job, and devoted herself to raising her family. Her two adult children, now employed and living independently, had long been Eva's main focus in life. Since her youngest left the household a year earlier, she had no one to take care of and her life suddenly seemed meaningless. Although Eva had drunk a lot for many years, after her last child left she began drinking earlier in the day and consumed considerably more. She was often intoxicated by early afternoon and had to take a nap. Afterwards she resumed drinking to get through the evening. Eva usually drank over a half gallon of wine every day and she felt terrible about herself and her drinking. She had tried cutting down but was unsuccessful.

Eva realized that she would have to make a pretty radical change in her lifestyle to get a handle on her drinking. She knew she missed having her kids around, but it was obvious she couldn't do anything about that. She hadn't worked for so many years that she wondered if she could even get and hold a job. But something big had to happen if Eva was going to conquer booze. Controlling it seemed out of the question. When she thought seriously about how wine affected her, she realized it only made her feel less bad, rather than good. Her life was simply not satisfying. Wine was like a sedative that provided escape. Since she had tried and failed several times to cut down, she finally decided to go cold turkey.

First, Eva got rid of all the liquor in the house. She went out and found a job at minimum wage as a clerk in a variety store. Despite the low pay, the job made her feel much better about herself and at the same time kept her busy and away from the bottle. She enjoyed being around other adults during the day. Evenings at home were her major hot spot, but Eva recruited the assistance of her husband, who was more than willing to help. At first they got out of the house a lot—movies, dinner, visiting nondrinking friends—and eventually, best of all, she and her husband started bowling again almost every night. They soon made new nondrinking friends. Within six months the rewards of her new, sober lifestyle made her as happy as she had ever been.

Self-change like Eva's does happen. But it's a lot easier if you have some specific guidelines such as those we will give you in this chapter.

MOTIVATION TO QUIT

Reread Chapter 9, "Motivating Yourself." If you are currently drinking, do the drinking session to obtain motivational pictures and sound recordings of your drunken behavior. Get that gut-level commitment from yourself with pictures of loved ones expressing their love or admonishing you to stop drinking. Whether or not you are still drinking, make a list of reasons to quit and a description of your drunken self to carry around with you. Post the pictures, lists, and descriptions in places where you need them the most to help you refrain from drinking. Be sure to have motivational materials along in case you come close to a hot spot. Use them *before* you enter the hot spot. Better yet, don't go near any hot spots. Assume you do not have an iron will and that you will need every break and motivational assistance you can arrange. Ultimately, it's up to you. *You* have to do these things and take sole responsibility for the change to a sober way of life. But you can make it easier for yourself and greatly increase your chance of success if you prepare and use these motivational boosters.

Target a date for quitting. Before then, do what this chapter says so you will be both motivated to quit and prepared to stay dry by knowing just how you are going to do it.

HOT SPOTS

Don't go near them if possible. All risks under your control should be eliminated, and your personal hot spots are prime risks. Favorite bars, heavy-drinking friends, parties—take them out of your life for now. Maybe you can put some of them back in later, but not until you are happy with the sober life. If your hot spot is at home, get rid of all your booze. Get out of the house as much as possible and especially at those times of day that are most troublesome (as Eva did). If you are not working, maybe you need a job to keep you from temptation and increase your self-respect as well. Or maybe you need to consider moving. Think radically and creatively about solutions to your hot spots.

CHANGE YOUR LIFESTYLE

You are going to be a different person in some important ways when you quit drinking. You must convince yourself and others that you are a nondrinker. You don't drink at all anymore and you mean it. If you are comfortable with it, declare your new nondrinking status loud and clear—especially to those who don't want you that way. Reread Chapter 11, "Handling Pressures." Write out your own script for refusing drinks and establishing yourself as a nondrinker. Practice your lines until you can say them as convincingly as a professional actor or actress. Be *proud* of yourself for being a nondrinker.

If you are not willing to let others know that you have had a drinking problem, then at least have your lines down pat for refusing drinks. A high level of performance is essential. Our view is that being a nondrinker should be as easy as being a nonsmoker in social situations. Of course it isn't yet, but if you can convince yourself of your absolute right not to drink, that will make it easier. If you are a nonsmoker and someone offers you a cigarette, it's easy to say "No thanks, I don't smoke." Try "No thanks, I don't drink." And *repeat it as many times as necessary without giving any reason or explanation.* Just repeat it. You have no obligation to anyone to account for yourself. You just don't drink. Often those who encourage you to drink do not have your best interests at heart anyway. They really don't care one way or the other about your personal welfare. So take responsibility for yourself and say you don't drink. Any other strategies, like turning your wine glass over (just as some people do their coffee cup), can also be used to get the message across clearly and prevent you from dealing with an unwanted glass of wine. But should you get one anyway, just leave it or offer it to someone else who won't hassle you about it.

If you have personal problems that are bothering you, consider getting professional help. Often such problems contribute to the abuse of alcohol and relieving them could make it easier to quit drinking and enjoy life a lot more. You can contact your local psychological association for possible names, or just check the yellow pages. A behavior therapist is more likely to be in accord with the methods of this book. If you go to a physician or psychiatrist for help, there is a good possibility that you will be given drugs as part of your treatment, something we often consider questionable since the abuse of a drug is already part of the problem. You can also call your local mental health association, the nearest community mental health clinic, or the psychology department of a nearby college or university. Often community-sponsored clinics charge fees on the basis of your ability to pay, so no one need feel unable to afford psychological counseling.

When you do get in touch with a specific therapist, never hesitate to ask what that person's orientation is, how much they will charge, what they intend to do for you, and what their qualifications are. If you start therapy and find that the therapist's attention is directed toward long, drawn-out discussions about your parents and childhood, find another. If the therapist tends to say nothing, but sits back and merely listens, refusing to suggest new strategies of behavior to help you be more effective, then we again suggest that you look further. Some therapists purposely avoid intervening in your life or changing anything, and we believe that most people go to a therapist for change. So if you are paying for change, why not get it? Finally, if for any reason at all you are not fully confident about a therapist, if you don't like his or her methods, mannerisms, fees, or pictures in the office, remember that you are employing him or her and not vice versa. Find someone you like and can work with, not somebody you clash with, so you can get into your personal problems and do something about them.

Alcoholics Anonymous or other alcohol-related groups and organizations might improve your enjoyment of life and pave the way for a life of contented, lasting sobriety. Look into them to see if they can make it easier for you. *Feel free to experiment without committing yourself.* You can easily visit and check out any group. If it's not what you expected, you do not have to continue.

ALTERNATIVES TO DRINKING

We have touched on some possible alternatives in our discussion so far, and we want to emphasize their importance here. You are not very likely to succeed with abstinence unless you find satisfying ways to fill in the time once spent on drinking. You must be happy to succeed in the long run. Chapter 12 tells you how to find alternatives and put them into your life. The bonus for the abstainer is overindulgence in alternatives. You may have to overdo it, just as you may have to be extreme in some other ways to get off and stay off booze. So lay in a tempting supply of your favorite nonalcoholic beverages, your favorite foods, and acquire those adult toys you've thought about and wanted but never allowed yourself to have. If you're not drinking, chances are you can afford to travel more, buy a new bicycle or a boat, go out to the better restaurants, see the latest movies, etc. Don't just give yourself grudging permission to do these things—they are *essential*. Being sober could be the best chance you've ever had to savor some of the good things in life you have wanted but denied yourself. You can avoid hot spots and enjoy being sober at the same time.

ERNIE THE NEWLY RICH

Ernie drank half a bottle of expensive whiskey every day. In addition, he made about ten visits to a public bar during the month, where he indulged freely and sometimes bought drinks for others. Ernie figured the 15 bottles he bought each month cost him $8 each for a total of $120 per month. He estimated his bar visits at $10 each, which amounted to another $100. Once he went cold turkey and quit drinking, Ernie was able to afford some great new pleasures with the additional $220 he saved each month. And Ernie was smart enough to spend it on activities and gifts to himself which helped a great deal in remaining sober and feeling good about it.

TWO STEPS FORWARD, ONE STEP BACKWARD

The nature of learning involves the possibility of temporary failure. Human beings naturally learn from mistakes, and that's just what we recommend that you do. Should you slip, don't condemn yourself as a failure. Look at failures as just a temporary part of the learning process. Pick up, start again, identify where you slipped up, examine the circumstances, find the previously unidentified hot spot, and benefit from this analysis of your slip-up to improve in the future.

Don't use the cop-out "loss of control" as an excuse for getting drunk. If you have a drink or two for whatever reason, you *can* stop right there. A little slip isn't as bad as a big slip. The traditional loss-of-control notion says that once you have started to drink you will experience an insatiable craving for more alcohol ("one drink, then drunk"). This myth has provided an excuse for many abusers to get drunk, as if drinking is completely out of their hands. One drink and abusers become the poor victims of a disease process over which they have no voluntary control, like cancer. But research has shown this notion to be false. Abusers *can* stop drinking once they have started, if the desire is there. That's why we tell you to carry with you some additional reminders that motivate you to quit drinking and stay that way (pictures, etc.). Pull them out if you've been drinking and *stop drinking* then and there. If you are looking for a miracle cure to stop drinking, you won't find it. There is no surgical procedure, no substitute drug, no magic person or group that will cause you to stop drinking. It's not like having your appendix out or a broken arm set. It cannot be hypnotized away. The only one who can do it is *you*, and it will take time and effort.

MARIO'S SETBACKS AND EVENTUAL SUCCESS ═══

Mario was a very serious abuser—he drank more than a fifth of hard liquor every day for many years. Mario thought of himself as an "alcoholic" and believed what he heard it meant. For example, once he started drinking he believed he would be unable to stop. Worse yet, he felt that one setback meant he was a total failure. These beliefs made it very hard for Mario to control his drinking. He had stopped many times only to start again after one episode of drinking. He said to his wife and friends, "I'm an alcoholic and I'm never going to change. Alcohol is poison to me. Once I start, I can't stop. Many times I've tried to stop and failed. So what's the use?"

But Mario was also intelligent, and logical. When he analyzed the argument that drinking is a disease, he found that it didn't make sense to him. His compulsion to drink was no more than the worst of bad habits. And he had gotten control of other bad habits like smoking and overeating. Why should drinking be any different? When losing weight, he had often slipped up by eating more than he should, and sometimes even gone on an eating binge. Yet the next day he redoubled his efforts and continued to diet successfully. Why should his drinking be any different? Mario decided that it wasn't. When he reflected on his drinking honestly, he realized that he had been using the label "alcoholic" to excuse himself from his failures. He went right back to drinking because he told himself that he was an alcoholic and had lost all control over his drinking. He finally decided that the road to abstinence might be fraught with the same kind of potholes as the road to losing weight. Nobody is perfect, and very few people make dramatic changes all of a sudden. So if he should get drunk after a period of sobriety, it didn't mean that he was a total failure. It meant instead that he would have to figure out what went wrong, correct it, and try even harder in the future. And if for any reason he should have a couple of drinks, he *could* stop. It was up to him.

Mario grew to accept setbacks as part of the learning process. He just wanted to see progress, with his failures decreasing in frequency and seriousness while his periods of sobriety increased. It took Mario nearly three years to remain completely sober for six months straight, but he did it. In his own mind, if he slipped up again at any time, despite his best efforts, he would avoid punishing himself for it, examine what went wrong, try to correct it, and carry on with renewed effort.

The thing that's going to keep you successfully sober is happiness. Most of what we've said is aimed at helping you deal with problems that prevent you from enjoying the sober life and enjoying it to the fullest. And we believe that's the key to lasting sobriety. Pursue happiness with vigor and remain on guard about your drinking. Thomas Jefferson once said, "Eternal vigilance is the price of peace." Well, eternal vigilance is also the price of lasting sobriety.

A SUMMARY OF THE STEPS TO SOBRIETY

You will have to be highly and consistently motivated to quit drinking and stay that way. Here's how to do it:

1. Above all, get motivated and stay motivated to stop drinking and remain sober so you can enjoy the good life.
2. Target a date for stopping.
3. Plan to change your lifestyle radically. Think of yourself as a nondrinker and be proud of it.
4. It is more difficult at first, so make it as easy as possible for yourself. At first, and maybe forever, get rid of all the alcoholic beverages in your house.
5. Avoid your hot spots completely.
6. Become as good as a professional actor or actress in assertively refusing drinks and establishing your role as a nondrinker.
7. Cultivate the best and most satisfying alternative activities to drinking that you can come up with. Use the money you are saving on booze to do this.
8. Consider professional therapy if you have personal problems.
9. Go to AA if their approach is compatible with your personality and beliefs.
10. Do not punish yourself for a setback. Study your mistakes, correct them, and redouble your efforts for success.

11. Reward yourself for your success. In addition to self-praise, spend the saved money to buy and do those things that will enhance the quality of your life.
12. Be on guard about your drinking at all times.

15

Putting It All Together

We began this book with a look at Mark, a moderate daily alcohol abuser who was then left in limbo to consider the methods that could be used to his advantage. Let us now return to Mark, see how he applied the steps to successful drinking in his life, and then summarize those steps.

MARK REVISITED

Mark began by learning the facts about alcohol. He was surprised to discover that not everyone regards alcohol abuse as a disease. Mark agreed that it was more logical to consider excessive drinking a bad habit just like the bad habits of overeating and smoking. He was especially interested in finding out that some problem drinkers can successfully learn moderation and get their drinking under control. He was interested to learn that the positive effects of alcohol occur when the BA is rising and that limiting himself to a peak BA of about 55 avoided the negative effects. Mark felt he could probably learn alternatives if he were more motivated and could reschedule his day to drink enjoyably when he did drink.

Mark's motivation came partly from his drunk driving conviction—a humiliating and expensive experience he definitely wanted to avoid repeating. Nevertheless, his drinking had returned to drunk-driving levels within just a few months after his arrest. Mark's awareness of this rather rapid increase to heavier drinking worried him. He needed to be better motivated to change his drinking habits. He agreed to let his wife take pictures of him as he became quite intoxicated one night after the kids were in bed. Photos taken early in the evening were not so bad or embarrassing. But later shots caught Mark sprawled out, groggy, on the couch. Closeups revealed a tired and older-looking face. One stunning shot captured Mark in the act of throwing up! This one was most arousing and upsetting to him. Looking at these photos while sober helped him develop a much stronger emotional commitment to change than he had previously been able to muster. Also, a tape recording of Mark's speech over the course of the evening revealed changes which he was surprised and embarrassed to hear. He found he could not count backwards from 100 by 7s. He could barely count backwards by 3s, and muttered forlornly, "How about by one's?" His speech was very slurred, tongue-twisters were almost unintelligible, and he sometimes lost his train of thought in the middle of a sentence. He was unable to say or write the alphabet in correct order. During the "drunk session" Mark considered his performance to be much better than it actually was. He insisted he would remember everything later, but his memory the next day was sketchy for much of the evening and absent for the last hour.

Mark pinned a closeup of his drunken face inside the liquor cabinet door to serve as a constant reminder to control his drinking. In his wallet he kept the shot of himself throwing up, for private viewing when he needed a motivational booster.

Mark began carefully recording his drinking and posted a graph of daily consumption on the inside of his bedroom door, a spot where visitors would be unlikely to see it. Since he weighed 160 pounds, his typical weekday consumption of 8 ounces of 80-proof Scotch over a two-hour drinking period (uninterrupted by dinner) was bringing him to a BA of about 110. His weekend daily drinking of 12 ounces over three to four hours was resulting in a BA of 170! The weekend amount was not only more excessive but usually made him feel very sleepy and "burned out." This kept Mark from more active, pleasurable, and definitely healthier activities.

Mark carefully considered his drinking records and examined the consequences of his drinking, concluding that he was a moderate abuser. Among the consequences indicating a genuine problem were fights with his wife when drinking, a poor sex life, his job performance suffering somewhat from irritability and lack of alertness during mild morning hangovers, his drunk driving conviction, frequent heartburn and stomach problems, and guilt over not having the pep or inclination to interact more with his kids. The cost of alcoholic beverages was not making a big dent in his income, but it was obvious that some of the money could be spent on better forms of entertainment.

The high-risk drinking times were found to be mainly after work on weekdays and midafternoon until bedtime on weekends. Mark established some practical guidelines to reduce his risk of drinking too much. For example, when he got home from work he made himself a large, *nonalcoholic* drink to quench his thirst and to satisfy his long-standing habit of carrying a drink around with him as he changed his clothes and settled down with the newspaper. After that nonalcoholic refresher was gone, he mixed a drink with a measured 1¼ ounces of Scotch and sat with his wife, and sometimes the kids also, to chat about their day. This time was planned for relaxation and was not to be spent solving problems (serious business being reserved for mornings, or after dinner if pressing). The "drinking period" was limited to a maximum of one hour and the Scotch to 3 drinks. This would provide a rising BA, with its attendant benefits, up to about 50. While drinking, Mark paid careful attention to the effects and avoided anything requiring responsible action, such as unwanted phone calls or unpleasant chores. He just enjoyed the good feelings of mild mood elevation and relaxation. Then dinner followed for everyone and usually ended the drinking period for that day.

Weekend days were somewhat more lenient, but prolonged drinking periods were avoided just as for weekdays. When they had company, Mark never took a drink before the guests arrived. Nor did he drink before going out to visit someone else.

With this new drinking style, Mark discovered that his energy level was usually sufficient to permit more active forms of play, often with his kids, such as shooting baskets, throwing a ball or frisbee around, riding a bicycle, or taking a walk after dinner. Sometimes they even did these things before dinner in place of the cocktail hour. Also, he and his wife made a point of getting a babysitter more often and going out to dinner or a movie or visiting friends. These expenses could easily be justified because less money was being spent on liquor. They were rewards for controlling his drinking. Mark and his wife made some new friends who were light drinkers and who enjoyed activities they had again picked up, including golfing, bowling, hiking, playing cards, and boating. Mark noticed that his wife was also drinking less. This change made him feel good because he no longer was a bad influence on her. Their sex life was better, too.

Mark developed his own rules for drinking, which he carefully followed. He would drink only from 5:30 to 6:30 on weekdays. He used his script for declining drinks with business associates after work, his major trouble spot besides home. Dinner was routinely served after a maximum of one hour of drinking (to no more than 55 BA). Mark and his wife discovered that they liked having dinner together as a family, especially since they still got to enjoy each other's company alone later in the evening now that Mark no longer routinely fell asleep from overdrinking. Naturally, working free of hangovers, Mark was more effective on the job.

Mark became skillful at deep-muscle relaxation, using the techniques we have described, helping him settle down into a more restful evening mood. When he drank, he got more out of it because he didn't use alcohol to get himself relaxed, but only to heighten his pleasant mood. Mark practiced enjoying the positive effects of alcohol by tuning in to them and savoring them as his BA was rising. He learned to really reserve his drinking time for pleasure, and not to be distracted by business or other responsible activities.

Naturally, Mark was used as an example in this book because he was so successful in turning around his drinking problem. But when the payoff from a change in lifestyle is great, the change usually lasts. Mark's life became so much better after controlling his drinking that it is unlikely he will return to his former abusive drinking habits. If you or someone close to you has a drinking problem, we sincerely hope that with the help of this book changes *can* be made and the problem brought under control.

SUMMARY OF THE STEPS TO SUCCESSFUL DRINKING

1. *Know the facts about alcohol.* You have an advantage if you understand how alcohol affects your body and behavior. For example, you can control your drinking more easily if you know how much alcohol is in various beverages and how much a person your size can drink over time and remain below a blood alcohol (BA) of 55. Understanding how alcohol affects your sleep, your sex life, your work, your social behavior, and your driving will pave the way for enjoying the benefits of drinking without experiencing any bad effects.

2. *Drink-watch.* While you nurse one, note how others seem to enjoy the benefits of a rising BA up to 40 or 50 for an hour or so. They begin to show negative effects above a BA of 55—uncontrolled emotions such as anger or depression, lack of awareness, poor coordination and speech.

3. *Drink-watch yourself.* Be aware of the effects of alcohol. Use the bodily sensations checklist to identify cues related to a moderate BA, such as feelings of warmth, a pleasant mood change, or changes in speech. Practice drinking and being aware of the effects of alcohol. Savor the good feelings as your BA is *rising,* when you get the most positive effects (*not* when your BA has stabilized, exceeds 55, or is falling). Don't do anything like mow the lawn or make important telephone calls when you drink. These distract from the good feelings you should be experiencing—after all, that's why you are drinking in the first place! In the early stages of training yourself to increase your enjoyment from drinking, plan special times to practice under ideal conditions such as at home in the evening. Like anything else, successful drinking takes practice, so when you drink, try to drink right.

4. *Evaluate your drinking.* Determine your intake. Keep a record of every drink you take. Just as a successful dieter charts daily calorie intake and weight, make a graph of your daily alcohol consumption. Your drinking record and analysis of the consequences of your drinking can be used to decide if alcohol is a problem for you and, if so, how much of a problem. Your drinking record will also allow you to watch your progress and identify hot spots where you tend to drink too much.

5. *Set limits.* Determine from the tables at the end of the book how many drinks you can have in an hour and stay below a BA of 55. To do so avoids practically all of the negative consequences, whether legal, vocational, economic, marital, physical, social, or personal. Yet you can still enjoy the positive results of drinking, such as forgetting your work for a while or tuning in to good feelings and good things in life more easily. Be gradual in reducing your intake to arrive at your final goal, and don't punish yourself for a slip-up now and then. Just keep at it.

6. *Get support from family and friends.* This is possible only if they can be supportive and nonjudgmental. Others who care can reward you with praise and encouragement as well as favors and gifts for making gradual progress. They can make it easier for you to be emotionally expressive and assertive, and to have a good time while sober. But they must not punish or confront you for setbacks lest they take away your exclusive responsibility for yourself and your drinking.

7. *Motivate yourself.* Heightening your motivation may require a bit of ingenuity in order to determine what works best for you. Display photographs taken while drunk—snapshots that are really upsetting to look at. Examine your self-prepared list of reasons to stop or reduce your drinking, and a description of your intoxicated behavior. Carry the list and description with you and read it over several times a day. A photo of a loved one, captioned "Please don't drink," "Take care of yourself for me," or "I love you" may work for you. If you are fortunate enough to have access to a home video system with camera, make a "drunk tape" and review it weekly.

8. *Manage hot spots.* Certain times, settings, and people may be

associated with excessive consumption. If you tend to drink too much early in the evening, then be ready with specific strategies to counter excessive tendencies at that time. It might help to have plenty of tempting nonalcoholic beverages around or to eat a delicious dinner soon after you arrive home. Perhaps something physical like swimming, tennis, or jogging early in the evening will settle you down and make it easier for you to control your drinking. The main thing is to be aware of your high-risk drinking situations and know what to do to avoid them or enjoy them without later on suffering the consequences of excess.

9. *Handle pressure effectively.* Learn to refuse drinks assertively. Know when and how to resist social pressure from others by politely but firmly turning down drinks. Rehearse your lines, borrowing from our suggestions or using your own self-written script. Depending on who is offering you a drink, and the degree of encouragement or even pressure, your assertive refusal may range from something like "No, thank you" or "Thanks, I'm fine," to a firm "I don't want one," or even "No, I'm definitely not going to have another drink!" Be prepared to repeat your refusal several times in a strong and convincing voice, looking the person in the eye so they get the message that you mean it.

10. *Establish alternatives to drinking.* Reconsider past hobbies you enjoyed, survey present interests, and consider some new fun things to do in place of drinking. Give preference to activities that serve the same purpose as alcohol. For example, if shifting gears to a more relaxed evening mood is something alcohol does for you, try instead shifting by doing something you also find relaxing, like playing racquetball, reading, walking, or even eating right away.

11. *Get mellow without alcohol.* Learn to relax to control tension and anxiety. Being able to relax voluntarily is a skill you can learn just like typing or riding a bike. It is a big advantage to be able to relax without using alcohol. You probably won't feel a need for as much alcohol if you drink only when you are already relaxed. Then you start out in a physical state that takes best advantage of the good feelings produced by drinking.

12. *Rehearse your drinking controls.* Spend five minutes early in

your day, and also just before entering any high-risk drinking situation, rehearsing the guidelines for controlling your drinking. Have a plan of action. Know how many drinks are your limit; be prepared to stop there. Rehearse your lines for refusing drinks in case you have to. Think of yourself as an actor or actress who is very well rehearsed before stepping onto the stage in your new role as "the successful drinker."

13. *Use the money you save from buying less liquor to reward yourself.* Go to more movies or plays, take trips, eat out, buy new clothes, etc.

14. *Reschedule your day to take advantage of your newly developing skills and pleasures.* Certainly you should enjoy drinking when you do it, but drink within your limit and schedule other activities besides drinking. And don't drink every day since after a while you may need more to get the effects you want (tolerance increases). Rehearse your drinking guidelines at the beginning of each day and before any drinking occasion, refuse drinks assertively, indulge yourself in constructive and fun alternatives to drinking, and plan your day around nondrinking activities.

15. *Think of yourself as a successful drinker.* Include everything you have learned about successful drinking into your self-image. Instead of putting yourself down, recognize that you now know your limits, are more aware of how much you have had, how high you feel, when and how to refuse more. Feel good about yourself. It's nice to be a successful drinker.

Problem-free drinking is possible if you conscientiously follow these guidelines and put forth the effort. You and your loved ones will all benefit. You will do better at your job and in your social life. You will be physically healthier, will like yourself better, and will enjoy life more!

PART III

Successful Drinking and Society

EVERY SOCIETY IN which alcohol is consumed has to deal with a variety of resulting social and personal problems. We must look realistically at these problems and make rational plans for the future. The fact that alcohol and gasoline do not mix poses great hazards to life, limb, and property in a world so dependent on the private automobile. The United States is experiencing a "get-tough" approach to drunk drivers, and the person who drinks and drives should be well aware of the many risks involved. In a society that encourages alcohol consumption, parents cannot avoid the question of what to teach their children about alcohol. We find the present haphazard alcohol education system for young people woefully inadequate, and suggest some basic changes. Finally, no book on alcohol would be complete without speculation about the future, so we gaze into our crystal ball and make some predictions. We conclude that our future will be much brighter if we recognize both the personal and societal responsibilities for the use of alcohol and emphasize alcohol education, prevention of abuse, and early intervention for developing problems.

161

16
Gasahol

Have you or a friend ever been arrested for drunk driving? The reality of that experience is often not at all what folks imagine it might be. In fact, it will come as a rude shock.

OBLIVIOUS DON

Don was driving home late one night after a very successful business conference. He was a real estate broker who had just put together a package for a new commercial development. That evening he had cleared the last hurdles with city management and was feeling particularly good about himself and the world. Don had also been drinking at the meeting, and the combination of his high spirits and bottled spirits resulted in a rather heavy foot on the gas pedal of his Mercedes–Benz. Even the red lights of the patrol car couldn't puncture his good mood—he felt confident that he could talk himself out of anything. After all, wasn't he the Supersalesman of the Decade?

Don spoke with assurance to the officer who came to his window. "Good evening. Did I make some kind of silly mistake back there?" The officer smelled his potent breath while leaning over the open car window. He asked Don to step out of the car. Don climbed out, still not worried since he didn't feel drunk, and got out his wallet and license. The officer was joined by his partner, and after checking Don's driver's license and car registration they put him through a sobriety test. He was instructed to write out the alphabet beginning at K. He couldn't. Then they had him stand on one foot, arms outstretched, with his head thrown back. He almost fell over. Don laughed it off, insisting that he was plenty sober enough to drive. "Hey, guys, I'm just on my way home from a meeting with the mayor and two city councilmen . . . your bosses, you know . . . and the city attorney too. I think it would be best for everybody involved if I just continued on my way home."

His "Don't you know who I am?" attitude had remarkably little impact on the patrolmen. They unsympathetically informed him that he would have to go with them to the station for further tests. Don was outraged. A man of his position being treated like this! He informed the officers that they were taking their careers into their hands with this action, and angrily told them, "You bastards better change your minds on this right now!" To his amazement, they grabbed him, spun him around, had handcuffs on him in a flash, and threw him roughly into the back seat of their patrol car. They called a tow truck for his car and drove him to the station while he loudly protested all the way. Upon arrival, he was manhandled into the station, where nobody listened to his loud protests. He found himself treated "like a piece of meat." He then had to blow into a breath machine, still arguing that he did not need testing, but cooperating rather than automatically losing his license. The reading was 120, above the 100 required to be convicted for drunk driving in California. Don protested that he wasn't drunk. They ran a second test which confirmed the first. He was then booked, fingerprinted, and thrown into the "drunk tank" with a batch of unsavory characters. The toilet was near overflowing, the place stank, and the mattress smelled like vomit. Don was also aware that he was getting funny looks from his cellmates and that scared him. He felt humiliated, infuriated, and helpless. He stood at the bars and hollered for the jailers—but was ignored. Don spent the next nine hours in jail, was finally released on his own recognizance, his wrists still sore from the cuffs. Before he could drive home he had to cough up $90 to release his impounded car.

Don's attorney told him there was no chance of beating the

charge, that plea-bargaining was no longer allowed in California drunk-driving cases. He ultimately had to accept the conviction, pay a large fine, spend two more humiliating days in the county jail, and attend a year-long program at Alcoholics Anonymous as a condition of probation (which also angered him since he denied being an alcoholic). His arrest appeared in the papers, he missed work during his two days in jail, and got lots of ribbing from colleagues and friends. To cap it off, he soon got a notice from his insurance company that his car premiums had been doubled. All of this because of his impaired judgment and reduced sensitivity to his real level of blood alcohol, and a choice to drink without having given it any thought before or after drinking.

The interesting thing about this case is that Don's experience is *not* unusual. It is routine for the police to make a drunk-driving arrest a terrible experience. We have heard many a horror story about being arrested for driving under the influence and cannot recall a single account in which it wasn't worse than expected. It's *always* bad. Even doctors and lawyers are humiliated with the same authoritarian domination as anyone else. Imagine being handcuffed and forced into the back seat of a police car! This is standard practice. It happens to everyone. Imagine being "in custody," a *prisoner* under the *physical control* of armed men who take your personal belongings and then put you in a barred cell and lock the door to keep you there like a caged animal—a danger to others who must be protected from you because you're drunk and not able to act responsibly. In addition, it usually smells bad in jail, nobody listens to you, and your fellow jailbirds are often frightening characters. And *should* you protest, "I'm a lawyer," or "You bastards are gonna pay," things get *worse* instead of better!

The sad stories we've heard! The lawyer who said he was going to sue: His handcuffs were painfully tightened and he was kept longer as a result. The affluent businessman who argued that he wasn't drunk and was subjected to extra "hands-on" treatment to "assist" him in and out of the police car and the drunk tank. The woman who was "strip-searched" for resisting arrest and cursing the police. It is quite apparent that society doesn't like drunk drivers and has authorized law enforcement officers to get the message across. Personally, we encourage you to believe the message secondhand rather than find out the hard way.

Many, if not most, drinkers will admit that at some time in their life they have driven a motor vehicle while intoxicated. The later realization that "I should never have been at the wheel" tells us little except to illustrate how thoroughly our judgment can be impaired while drinking. The only difference between all those drinkers who have driven after "one too many" without incident and those who ended up in trouble is simple luck. Any occasionally driving drinker who tut-tuts when a prominent citizen is arrested for drunk driving is simply being a hypocrite. It could just as well have been him.

We all know that drinking and driving do not mix. Someone is killed in a drunk-driving accident in the United States every 23 minutes; the annual total is over 26,000! If a small town with that population were wiped out in an explosion, it would be considered the worst disaster in United States history—yet one by one we hardly notice. More than a million Americans a year suffer serious and often crippling injuries in drunk-driving incidents. The direct cost of this problem is more than $5 billion annually. For Americans up to age thirty-five, motor vehicle accidents are the number one cause of death, and more than half are the result of drunk driving. It is estimated that on the average weekend night, one out of every 10 drivers on the road is drunk. Try playing "drunk spotter" next time you are out driving on a Friday or Saturday evening. Watch as the police do for cars with tires riding the lane marker, weaving, making wide turns at intersections, stopping well before a light, or even driving so slowly as to be a hazard.

We are all horrified by the stark reality of drunk-driving statistics. Yet for us simply to repeat these figures and exhort drinkers not to drive after indulging in alcohol will probably have no effect whatsoever. All drinkers *already know* they shouldn't drive—but they do. What we *can* do that might be of help is to suggest that drinkers should carefully *plan* their intake around driving, just as we have been encouraging them to do in relation to other parts of their lives. We think people should not drink at all if they are going to drive but, consistent with the practical orientation of this book, we must recognize that society *does* sanction drinking and driving up to a point (you are usually not convicted unless your BA is above a certain level or you are driving erratically). First we will look at the nature of driving impairment caused by drinking. Then we will consider some of the new and ever more serious consequences of a drunk-driving arrest and suggest some sensible guidelines to reduce risks.

If you do drink and drive, what are your chances of having an accident? It is estimated that 50 percent or more of all highway accidents involve a drinker who is under the influence of alcohol. But the probability of getting into a highway accident increases dramatically as a driver's blood alcohol increases. For example, the probability of causing a crash is 4 times greater at a BA of 100 as compared with a BA of under 30. At 150, the risk is 8 times greater than it is below a BA of 30. Most states require a BA of 100 for "driving under the influence," but because of the accelerating impairment above a BA of 50, we think that 100 is too lenient and strongly suggest a BA of 50, as it is in the state of Oregon, and in Sweden and Norway.

Unfortunately, one of the reasons people often drive while still intoxicated is that, like Don, they honestly feel more sober than their BA would indicate, an unhappy consequence of tolerance. Remember, you may feel almost sober but still have an elevated BA.

Drinking drivers have yet another problem. Because alcohol impairs vision, the drinking driver does not see everything as well as necessary for safe driving. Even small amounts of alcohol prolong recovery time from glare, resulting in a period of relative blindness. It becomes more difficult to adapt to variations in light, peripheral (side) vision is impaired, and visual search behavior is reduced. Nighttime driving therefore compounds the visual problems of driving under the influence, and drunk driving is more common at night. Naturally, alcohol's effect as a loosener of inhibitions is also likely to encourage the kind of reckless driving that leads to emergency situations which our bodies are then unable to handle.

Alcohol's sedative effect often results in feeling drowsy and falling asleep. One weekend, as we were working on the manuscript for this book, a prominent Sacramento man—a former county supervisor, advertising executive, and television personality—was found dead in his car. He was sitting parked in his closed garage at 7:30 A.M., the car engine still running. His blood alcohol level was found to be 180. Because of a history of falling asleep in his car in the driveway after returning home late, it appeared that this was no suicide. Instead, he probably drove into the garage, closed the door with the automatic door closer, and fell asleep before shutting off the car engine. The combination of alcohol and drowsiness cost him his life.

While coffee, a blaring car radio, or open windows may help a driver stay awake for a short period of time, such techniques are poor solutions to the problem when we consider the other alternatives available to the drinking motorist. Finding another way to travel the same distance without having to operate a motor vehicle in an intoxicated condition is the wise choice. (A drunk person waiting an hour before driving has achieved no real solution because the BA drops by only 15 per hour and the drinker, still drunk, may feel even more tired after the hour has passed.)

You will not be surprised to learn that as BA readings go up, reaction times become longer. However, judgments of all types also suffer. For example, one recent study found that a bus driver clearly took greater risks in navigating his bus between objects while intoxicated than when sober. Perhaps the basic miscalculation made by the intoxicated individual is the decision to operate a vehicle in the first place. In this regard, intoxicated motorists typically do not comprehend their handicap, and often act as if none existed at all.

Many of the unhappy occurrences related to alcohol and automobiles are similar to those in other social situations. In social relationships, as in cars, intoxicated persons tend to lose their inhibitions. More specifically, they become less concerned with the *consequences* of their actions, and forget or even ignore their previous social learning and normal controls. It is as if intoxicated people were behaving primarily in the "here and now" rather than in relation to past experiences or to future expectancies. Yet never has the drinker needed to be so aware of *consequences* as today, because they are changing at a rapid pace for drunk drivers. Booming new organizations around the country such as MADD (Mothers Against Drunk Drivers) and RID (Remove Intoxicated Drivers) are taking their concern to the legislatures and courts, and the result is stiff and unavoidable penalties for drinkers, as well as possible murder charges if someone is killed. These groups were formed by outraged citizens who had lost children or other loved ones to crashes caused by drinking drivers. Historically, death-dealing drunk drivers have often walked away with minor fines or penalties. In 1980, routine drunk drivers in New York paid an average $12 fine while individuals convicted of killing a deer out of season paid $1,500. New laws around the country are forcing rapid change. In California, a 48-hour jail term or drastic restriction of driving privileges is now mandatory for all drunk drivers. During the first month that law was in effect, drunk-driving arrests and alcohol-related traffic deaths dropped by more than 20 percent compared to the prior year. Judges are being monitored to ensure their taking a hard line with drunk drivers. New York now requires a minimum $350 fine for a first drunk-driving offense. Meanwhile, new bills are being proposed to Congress and the Senate that would impose mandatory sentences nationwide, additional imprisonment for repeat offenders, mandatory license suspension, and national coordination of laws with a national standard of 100 BA (which we think should be 50) as legally drunk. So, the loud and clear message is don't drink and drive, or at least drink very little if driving. Call a cab, let someone else drive, spend the night, do anything but get behind the wheel if you have had more than a small amount of alcohol. There are risks associated even with a BA of 30, and 55 is the upper limit to even consider driving in our opinion.

If you have a BA below 55 and you choose to drive, you ought to follow certain guidelines to reduce risks. Be sure you know your BA. Drive on familiar roads to minimize the possibility of the unexpected. Pay strict attention to the task of driving. Be assertive with those who would distract you, as your job is a matter of life and death to everyone on the road. But bear in mind that even if your BA is under 55, the roads are familiar, and you are concentrating on your driving, you may not be able to comprehend the significance of events or exercise sound judgment, and you may lack the coordination to drive safely even if you "feel" sober.

Indeed, someday historians may look back on today's drink-and-drive society and conclude that one of the dumbest sayings of all time was "Let's have one for the road!" That slogan probably got its start in the days of stagecoach travel when hot, rough, and dusty hours were well worth tuning out through alcohol. Next time you take a stagecoach, go right ahead and have "one for the road." But if you are going to travel by car, please skip the booze altogether, for your own sake and that of everyone else who shares the road.

17

Youth and Alcohol

To drink or not to drink is a primary question faced by young people. The reality and problem with young people and alcohol is that they ultimately make their own decisions about drinking. Regardless of school programs, TV shows, parental lectures, or exhortations from the pulpit, the bottom line is that teenagers themselves decide whether or not to drink. Equally important if they opt for drinking is that they must also decide when, where, and how much to drink. We think it is essential for parents to carefully consider how our youth arrive at these decisions and what society does and does not do to influence them. Unfortunately, a significant proportion of the adult population honestly believes that ignorance about sex, drugs, and alcohol is actually desirable and will somehow prevent young people from becoming interested in these forbidden fruits. Such parental attitudes are a major stumbling block to the development of effective alcohol education.

A poor alternative to ignorance has been use of the classic fear approach, the scare-the-hell-out-of-'em philosophy that was responsible for the absurd high school VD movies of the 1950s and the blood-and-guts crash films that sometimes still masquerade as "driver education." Scare tactics remain the basis for some present-day drug and alcohol programs for youth. There is a basic problem common to all scare approaches: Today young people often know that the exaggerated and sometimes preposterous events depicted are simply not true or realistic. Hundreds of thousands of young people have

171

laughed themselves to tears watching the film *Reefer Madness,* a 1930s morality play supposedly revealing the evils of marijuana, so idiotic in its warnings and characterizations that it has become a cult classic of bizarre entertainment. And when youngsters laugh at such films it is only natural for them to skeptically laugh at serious efforts to alert them to the hazards of drugs, whether marijuana, other illegal drugs, or alcohol, our favorite legal recreational drug.

In addition, children often see unrealistic drunks on stage or screen who are so burned out and enslaved by booze that their predicaments are a curiosity or even humorous rather than something with which they can sympathize. The main character of *Days of Wine and Roses,* the classic film about alcohol abuse, is so grotesquely out of control, so totally insane in his desire for a bottle, that the vast majority of young viewers simply cannot identify with him. It is very easy to cop out and label him a "nut" or a "wiped-out alky" and thereby conveniently ignore the message being presented. Playwrights and screenwriters are creative artists and their personal views of alcohol abuse may not correspond to the reality of what alcohol abuse is like for most abusers. Or else they are creating drama which makes its point at the expense of distorting the true nature of alcohol abuse. We believe that greater numbers of people would benefit if dramatic stories about alcohol abuse more closely conformed to the real-life problems of everyday abusers. Such abusers could then see themselves in the story and come away feeling that the message pertained to them—not to some pathetic, far-out alcoholic.

Let us make it clear that we are in no way advocating playing down the physical and social dangers of alcohol. They exist and should be presented to our youth in a straightforward manner. What we *are* saying is that young people today are too sophisticated to be influenced by unsophisticated scare tactics. One-sided presentations of any social problem, whether involving sex, drugs, tobacco, or alcohol, tend to be self-defeating because they turn off young people who can see through their basic dishonesty. An honest presentation of alcohol requires acknowledgment that drinking offers more than just dangers, or else half the world would hardly continue to drink.

Children can be told the reasons why some people choose to drink and why some do not. They can handle the facts, the pros and cons, if they are given basic information about the effects, the joys, and the sorrows of booze. It is only through such a presentation that young adults will be able to make informed, sensible choices.

RUDY LEARNS THE HARD WAY

Several of Rudy's sixteen-year-old buddies decided to throw a booze party and he was invited. They were going to use the house of a friend whose parents were out of town, leaving them free to live it up. Before the party a few of Rudy's chums were bragging about their drinking ability and how much they were going to drink. Rudy had never drunk more than a beer or two and wasn't sure whether or not he should go. There was no one he really trusted to ask about it, so he went to the party not knowing for sure what he would do. Naturally he succumbed to the pressure to drink and, after much encouragement from his friends, he decided to "go for it" with something strong, whiskey and 7–Up. His more experienced buddies gleefully mixed him a very strong drink and gave him another just as soon as he gulped down the first. Rudy had been sitting at a table and never got up until halfway through his third drink. He was totally surprised to find he could hardly walk. His skin was flushed, his speech thick, and his thinking power gone. In a few minutes, Rudy became nauseated and soon found himself with his head over the toilet. Since he had not eaten supper and had drunk very rapidly, he discovered the agony of the dry heaves, which was the last thing he remembered. Thinking coffee would sober him up, his friends tried to get several cups down him but he threw it back up, getting some on the carpet. His best friend, also inexperienced with booze and himself quite intoxicated, drove Rudy home but had a little trouble navigating their driveway and hit a fence. Rudy and his friend ended up in serious hot water with their parents.

All together, Rudy's first drinking episode was not enjoyable at all. He had not carefully thought beforehand about whether or not he should drink, instead letting his friends decide for him. He had no idea how much or how fast he could drink and enjoy it, and became ill and vomited on the carpet, which was embarrassing later. Transportation home was also disastrous and Rudy was sick the next day. He could have handled the situation much more successfully if he had had better information and an example of a successful drinker in his life. With a bit of help, he might have decided not to drink. Or if he decided to drink, he could have provided for his own safety by having a parent or sober friend pick him up and take him home at a reasonable hour. And certainly Rudy's rapid consumption could have been avoided with a little knowledge of the negative results of drinking too fast, especially on an empty stomach.

We are aware that some parents will disagree with an approach that acknowledges the pleasures of drinking and will argue that teenagers should simply be told "No!" and given no further information about alcohol. But if such an approach is taken, you can be assured that they *will* get "information" about alcohol and plenty of it, exactly as happens when sex education is ignored by schools and parents. And most of what they get will be of questionable value. We have already described in Chapter 2 the distorted TV presentation of drinking, graphically showing its use as an escape and promoting alcohol as sophisticated fun and the road to instant "macho." To these systematic inducements for young people to drink add the desire to be adult, pressure from drinking friends, teenagers' intense need to go along with the group, and you have very powerful training in *how to drink wrong.* In our opinion, it is this haphazard negative training in our society that has produced many of our adult problem drinkers, people who became drinkers largely through a series of accidental or unplanned events, who never really seriously looked at alcohol, considered the pros and cons, or made any kind of carefully considered decision. As educators, we assert that knowledge does *not* lead to abuse, but instead leads to intelligent decision-making, and we consider that preferable to letting the decision to drink be made by friends, movies, TV stars, or Madison Avenue sales pitches.

So what is the first step in rational alcohol education? *Give teens the honest pros and cons.* Why do people drink? Because it feels good, it pleasantly changes the state of consciousness. The fact that human beings around the world throughout history have amused themselves by altering their state of consciousness can and should be understood by children. Why do we deny this reality? Parents talking to children about sex often explain that people have sex to produce babies, when in reality, the main reason for most people is that sex feels good—something youngsters quickly discover for themselves whether adults say so or not. Similarly, drinkers like the way alcohol makes them feel. Acknowledge it and start from there.

What else? Alcohol seems to facilitate social events, helping us "relax and get loose." In addition, the flavor of various liquors appeals to some drinkers. Finally, having a drink serves for many as a kind of green light for good times, a cue to unwind, forget about work, enjoy social interchange, smile and laugh and have fun. These are the honest, primary, and realistic reasons why people drink.

Then let's give young people the reasons for either *not* drinking or carefully controlling intake. In this book we have explored a stack of negative consequences stemming directly from drinking. When taken in excess, alcohol can cause damage to the brain, liver, and heart. Drinking contributes heavily to traffic deaths and injuries, is involved in crime, marital problems, missed work because of hang-overs, financial strains on family budgets, child abuse, poor nutrition, and so on. Children need to know about these hazards, far greater in number than the benefits of drinking.

Perhaps more important, they should also be shown that if we take a close look at the positive consequences of drinking, we will find that it is actually possible to achieve every one of them in our daily life *without* alcohol. For example, there are various drug-free ways to pleasantly alter our state of consciousness. We can meditate, do deep-muscle relaxation, listen to our favorite music, enjoy a physical high through exercise, create new things with our hands, appreciate beauty by losing ourselves in a sunset or driving through a scenic val-ley, go to an exciting movie, ride a roller coaster, and even revel in the joys of delicious food. There are many ways to feel good and different that do not require booze.

What about our social functioning? Young people should know that it too can be facilitated in other ways. While it is true that a cocktail or two may make it easier for us to comfortably speak up in a group of strangers or approach a member of the opposite sex, the learning of social skills for effective conversation can have the same effect. We can master a variety of ways to be more comfortable expressing our ideas, meeting people, interacting with strangers, all without booze, and we may even be better at socializing because, when sober, we will pick up more accurate feedback about how we are doing and how others are reacting to us. (Remember, a drinker may feel witty and charming after a few drinks, but others may find him or her obnoxious.)

And what of the enjoyable flavor of alcoholic beverages? For most people this is entirely an acquired taste and does not come naturally. If a young person were purposely to avoid acquiring that taste, it would hardly be missed, as there are unlimited other fine food and drink flavors to keep the gourmet palate occupied and amused for longer than most of us have time on earth.

Finally, as far as a drink in the hand being a cue or signal for a good time, this clearly could just as well be served by almost any other cue to shift gears, from sitting down with the evening paper, to putting on casual clothes, eating some pretzels and drinking a diet soda, or flopping in front of the stereo and clamping on a set of earphones. In other words, alcohol is just one of many pleasurable options, and enjoyment of a rich life certainly does not hinge upon drinking. Young people should know these facts and have plenty of time to prepare for their own decisions, which they will inevitably make.

THOSE WHO DECIDE "NO"

Teens who conclude that drinking is not for them should be prepared by parents for intense pressure to change their minds. First, they should know how to assertively say no and make it stick, as described in our chapter, "Handling Pressures." It is important for nondrinking teens to tolerantly understand their drinking friends' curiosity and interest in alcohol, and not fall into the role of a "moral crusader" who tries to push a personal decision onto unwilling friends. Nobody becomes more of a target for pressure or hostility than the moralizing zealot. Nondrinking teens should practice telling people up front that they prefer not to drink, while making no big issue of it. At social functions they can drink nonalcoholic beverages and learn to fend off criticism in a good-humored way: "I'm trying to get into shape and booze slows me down." Nondrinkers must also be prepared to see their drinking friends become unusually emotional or aggressive, and even act in hostile or destructive ways that would never happen while sober. The nondrinker should be aware that he or she could be held partly responsible for what happens when socializing with drinkers. When it comes to driving, the nondrinkers must never be dependent for transportation on someone who will be drinking. That dependence could block a safe exit from a bad situation as well as expose one to the dangers of riding with a drunk driver. In short, nondrinking teens should be prepared to share the fun with drinking peers if it is safe, but also to exit gracefully if the situation gets dangerous or if they are targeted for insults, pressure to drink, or angry reprisals. Sometimes they may feel excluded or ostracized from a social situation because of their refusal to drink. Being prepared not to take it personally helps avoid the hurt of rejection that is so keenly felt by teenagers. Chances are that when the drinking friends are sober, things will be normal again (and the drinkers may even be embarrassed about their drunken behavior).

One way to minimize pressure on a nondrinking teenager is to make sure he or she is not the only abstainer at a social function. A friend can be taken if necessary. Social psychologists have demonstrated repeatedly that if a nonconformist has support from even one other person, such an ally greatly reduces the impact of group pressure. Besides, saying no has gained much support in recent years. A major segment of the population now chooses not to smoke and finally feels free to make that preference clearly heard and the right to that choice absolute. This militancy in freedom of choice makes it easier today to stick by the choice not to drink. In addition, the growing attention to physical fitness and health also adds support for the individual who chooses to forgo alcohol, just as it does for those who refuse cigarettes, French fries, or salt. There has never been a better time for young people to say no and be able to stick by their decision.

THOSE WHO DECIDE "YES"

We must accept the fact that some young people will decide that they want to experiment with alcohol. A valuable first step in sensibly working through that process is being able to talk honestly with a trusted and respected adult who drinks successfully. This could be a parent, teacher, aunt, uncle, or anyone who can be candid and open, and preferably comfortable to talk with. It can be invaluable for new drinkers to discuss openly with adults why they drink, what they drink, in which situations, what are the pros and cons as they see them, and how intake is controlled. Have they ever been in trouble while drinking? Have they had any problems with drinking too much? A respected adult who drinks successfully is an excellent source of information and a positive model.

From the start, parents should make their children aware of local laws about drinking and the penalties for underage use and possession. Many states have laws prohibiting open containers in automobiles, and teenagers are often unaware that a driver can be arrested just because a passenger has an open beer can.

Part of alcohol education for new drinkers must be an understanding of the realities of blood alcohol and tolerance. For the inexperienced it takes only a low BA like 20 to feel a real high. At 55 a new drinker may not be legally drunk, but could be markedly impaired even though at a blood alcohol level that is handled fairly well by experienced drinkers. The message is *be careful.* They should tune in to bodily feelings, gauge when they are high, and be ready to refuse more drinks despite pressure.

The "let's get drunk" approach to drinking is a common part of the youth culture. We have all heard young (and not so young) people brag about how much they drank at a party or over the weekend: "Boy, did we get smashed! I can't remember a thing!" There will be proponents of this philosophy of drinking at many teen parties and young drinkers should be ready to resist their urgings. The fact that some individuals' entire self-concept is tied to how much they can put away does not mean the others must follow suit. It is possible to say "Hey, get as smashed as you want, but don't expect me to."

Something else often ignored by adults is the fact that there will be times when curious young drinkers will knowingly choose to become drunk just to see what it is like. We often ask drinkers, "What do you want to achieve with your drinking?" They sometimes say things like "I want to get smashed, forget everything. . . . It's bombs awaaaaaaaaaay!" If that is the case, it is surely better to plan such a drinking episode safely than to just let it happen and suffer unexpected consequences. Regardless of age, if someone decides to get bombed, there are some obvious basic rules: (1) Don't drink in a car, don't drive after drinking. (2) Be careful in your choice of drinking partners, avoiding those who get "wild" and may carry out antisocial or destructive acts. (3) Have someone along who is sober and responsible (remembering that when it comes right down to it, nobody is responsible for you except yourself). (4) The ideal place to do it is where you can spend the night, and where no one who has been drinking needs to drive. Young drinkers should do it at home if their relationship with parents allows this level of honesty. (5) Be careful with your *rate* of drinking, even if you are trying to get drunk. Remember that every now and then newspapers carry a story about someone who chug-a-lugged a fifth of whiskey and promptly dropped dead. Alcohol is lethal if enough gets into the bloodstream. Also, if your blood alcohol rises too quickly, you (like Rudy) will throw up, hardly a fun part of anyone's day.

So watch the rate of drinking, monitor the total amount, be in a safe place, have a responsible and sober person present, and have transportation arranged beforehand. All of these arrangements will minimize the risk when someone purposely decides to get drunk.

Since many young adults are relatively naive about alcohol, we think they should do some of the same things that problem drinkers do to gain control of their drinking: First, watch other young folks drink, estimate their blood alcohol, and observe behavior changes. Under safe conditions they should carefully monitor their own intake, learn how to have an accurate idea of blood alcohol, and focus upon the changes and feelings, including the impairment of movement, speech, etc. They should always consider their reasons for drinking and have those reasons in mind when drinking. They can set limits for successful drinking (Chapter 7), keep track of the number of drinks consumed, and know how to refuse drinks. It is best to eat before or while drinking to avoid getting too intoxicated, drink for less than an hour, then stop drinking by doing something else that can safely be enjoyed. Young people always can consider alternatives to drinking and must keep in mind the legal consequences if under age.

We hope that someday realistic alcohol education and training for successful drinking will be made available for all young people who choose to drink. We would like to see such training offered for parents *and* their children, where together they could learn to accurately estimate blood alcohol, focus on the good feelings of a rising BA, and then turn off their interest in alcohol while devoting attention to alternative activities. This would go a lot farther toward promoting responsible adult drinking than does today's typical family situation with parents telling their teens "Don't you drink!" while demonstrating daily the very behavior they prohibit for their children. It's a simple reality that young people learn to do what they see us do, *not* what we tell them to do. If young people cannot learn nondrinking or successful moderate drinking from their parents or in their school, then where are they to learn it?

18

The Future

In our opinion we will see major changes in the years ahead as our society begins to understand alcohol use from a social learning perspective. Drinking is a *learned behavior*. Biological factors will be included in the learning account, but they will not occupy the central role they do currently. It may take some time, but the disease approach to alcohol abuse will lose favor because of the lack of evidence to support it.

There will be many benefits in this change of approach. Drinking habits will be measured along a continuum, i.e., in terms of degree of use. We will easily be able to determine how much of a habit any particular drinker has in comparison with others, and tell if and how much it is changing as time passes. Better tests for measuring drinking habits will be developed. For example, in our own laboratory we now have a measure of tolerance to the effects of alcohol that identifies for us the kind of drinking a given person does. The drinker need not tell us about drinking habits, because we automatically have a rather good idea of the extent of his or her drinking habit from the tolerance test alone. It will no longer be necessary to rely on the frequently distorted reports drinkers give about their drinking (either on purpose, because of poor memories, or from not paying attention to how much they drink). Eventually we will be able to correlate specific differences in alcohol use to other important life events such as health, personality factors, and social and cultural experiences, which will give us a better overall understanding of how alcohol affects our lives.

One big advantage of the learning approach and its emphasis upon measuring the degree of alcohol use is that we can identify changes in drinking and advise people to take corrective measures if their drinking indicates they are headed for trouble. The emphasis will someday be on *prevention* rather than treatment. We won't wait as we do now for problems to develop, nor until the situation becomes so severe that abstinence is the only effective solution. Many mild and moderate abusers will be able to *learn* moderation rather than try to deal with their drinking on their own, which too often fails. Society now offers virtually nothing for mild abusers. They must get worse first. But in the future, moderation will be available to them, and at a time when they can best use it. Serious abusers who can't drink, and those who for any reason choose not to drink anymore, will be able to learn a contented life of sobriety more easily with learning techniques than they can now, and without the stigma and degradation of being called an "alcoholic."

Alcohol education in the public schools will become common and more along the lines of what we've discussed in the previous chapter. The emphasis will be on a realistic and practical understanding of alcohol—its uses and misuses. The decision to drink or not to drink will be carefully considered, sensible guidelines for successful drinking will be provided for those who choose to, and the *prevention* of drinking problems will be among the major topics of alcohol education classes in schools.

Moderation training will be offered in community colleges, through other public school programs, and by private groups. Such programs will not compete with the valuable work of Alcoholics Anonymous, whose approach is mainly for the "bottomed-out" serious abuser anyway. Rather, they will extend help to the millions of unsuccessful drinkers whose problems with alcohol are not so severe, but who nevertheless need some assistance in controlling their habit.

Broad-spectrum help at many levels, as we are predicting, will also become a part of the insurance benefits offered through employers, who will find the cost-benefits of such help very advantageous ("profitable" is the word). Such benefits will make it possible for employees who would like to insure themselves against *becoming* abusers to attend workshops on successful drinking and how to maintain it. Others who may have some difficulty with alcohol will learn how to handle it before it creates major problems. The result will be better efficiency, reduced absenteeism, increased productivity and profits, and the improved welfare and happiness of employees. Progressive companies and unions that realize these advantages will doubtless be doing this within the next five years; some are doing it already.

All of the future changes we have discussed so far will be facilitated by the emerging technology of mechanical and electronic aids, especially blood alcohol monitoring devices. The widespread low-cost availability of blood alcohol measuring devices will help millions control their intake. Very few drinkers today know accurately what their actual BA level is while they drink, unless they find out the hard way from the police. But soon such devices will be as common and as inexpensive as electronic calculators. At present, Intoximeters, Inc.,* manufactures the hand-held Alco-sensor III for $420, which gives quick and accurate BA readings from breath samples. Continental Trading Corporation† markets the Swedish-made Alco–Check for $79, a similar portable breath-analysis device that gives BA ranges but not precise readings. The Alco–Check has a "traffic-light" display that indicates green for a BA of 0–50, amber for 50–100, and red for above 100. Just as the cost of calculators and digital watches has dropped from several hundred dollars to under $50, so will BA devices continue to become cheaper and more widely available. In the future drinkers will be able to check their BA at any time and any place. They can slow down or stop drinking when they should and make more responsible decisions about critical matters such as driving. Law enforcement people will be able to eliminate the Field Sobriety Test and simply take BA readings on the spot. The Los Angeles Police Department presently uses a BATmobile (Blood Alcohol Testing mobile) for field checks of suspected drunk drivers. But soon all police vehicles will be equipped with reliable

---

* Intoximeters, Inc., 1901 Locust St., St. Louis, Missouri, 63103.

† Continental Trading Corp., 6600 France Avenue South, Minneapolis, Minn., 55435. Phone: 612-920-0108.

breath alcohol-testing devices. This will solve the problem of failure to obtain convictions based on the argument that suspects' BAs at the time of arrest could have been below 100 and risen to above 100 by the time they were checked at the police station.

Bartenders and liquor store owners can resort to the objectivity of such breath alcohol machines rather than try to make an educated guess about whether or not to serve an intoxicated patron. Any employment situation involving public safety, such as the responsibility of airline pilots, bus drivers and train engineers, could be made safer by requiring routine quick and easy blood alcohol checks. But it is average drinkers, and those affected by them, who will benefit the most because they will more easily learn safe drinking limits.

In the future, society itself will assume more responsibility for how people drink rather than putting it entirely on the individual's shoulders. One of the good intentions of the disease approach to alcohol problems is to take some of the blame off individual drinkers by calling them the victims of a disease. As we thoroughly discussed in earlier chapters, the problem with this is the stigma of *accepting* the disease label, which most drinkers just won't do until they are in really bad shape. But another and better way of doing this will result from society itself taking some of the blame—and the responsibility for improving things. We think society and the individual share responsibility for abusive drinking. Our "wet culture" *can* make some changes in how it deals with drinking, such as requiring a BA of under 50 for automobile drivers. This change in Norway and Sweden, where violators are severely punished, has resulted in a reduction in the number of alcohol-related car accidents and other violations. We could close all bars and liquor stores during the 4–6 P.M. rush hour to eliminate one major social hot spot. Bartenders and liquor stores could be legally required to check the BA of patrons suspected of being too intoxicated. We could change alcoholic beverage advertising on radio and TV that misleads the public by associating drinking with success, riches, sex, and so on. Advertisements could instead show that successful drinking can enhance life in certain ways, such as at mealtime, but *not* suggest that drinking for its own sake or just to get drunk ("go for the gusto") is the way to drink. We believe that ads showing *responsible* drinking will be just as effective in selling the product, and at the same time contribute to, rather than detract from, the welfare of everyone. To its credit, the Distilled Spirits Council of the United States (DISCUS), which is supported by the liquor industry, already promotes sensible drinking through public-service media messages.

All alcoholic beverage containers should, and we think will, be required to indicate alcohol content (beer, ale, and malt liquor containers do not in most states at present). Moreover, every container should indicate the amount it takes to bring people to particular BAs. Aspirin and other nonprescription drug containers are required by law to indicate the therapeutic dose for the average adult and child. Something like the following example for 80-proof whiskey bottles would be very helpful in promoting responsible drinking:

SAFE INTAKE

The amounts of this beverage the average person (150 pounds) can consume in one hour and reach the blood alcohol levels shown below are:

BA of 20	BA of 40	BA of 60
2 oz.	3 oz.	4 oz.

Perhaps we are optimistic in predicting that movies and TV shows will become more realistic in their portrayal of drinking problems and possibly even show more people in appropriate, responsible drinking roles. By doing so, they would alert the public to the hazards of unsuccessful drinking in a believable way so that the jump to self-application can be made. Moviegoers can identify, and therefore see meaning for themselves, in films that portray unsuccessful drinkers who are very much like them, rather than characters who are far-out drunks with whom they cannot identify.

Finally, society will become more supportive in encouraging play and recreation, relieving some of the pressure produced by a compulsive-work philosophy and simultaneously decreasing the demand for alcohol to escape that pressure.

The future, in short, will offer better opportunity for living successfully with alcohol, enjoying its benefits, and avoiding its pitfalls.

While drinkers still have primary responsibility for arranging their environment and modifying their lifestyles to make drinking an acceptable and enjoyable part of life, society should acknowledge responsibility for its influence on drinking, and take an *active* role in fostering successful drinking habits and supporting the rights of those who choose not to drink.

The Scientific Basis for This Book

THE IDEAS ABOUT drinking in this book are based on over fifteen years of clinical practice and experimental research by the authors, plus a comprehensive knowledge of others' work through the scientific literature. Since 1967 we have received grants to support our alcohol research from state, federal, and private sources in excess of $1 million.

In our initial research we assumed nothing about the nature of drinking behavior except that learning probably plays a significant role, as is true in general for human behavior. We set about exploring the effectiveness of various techniques for changing drinking habits, including aversion conditioning, videotaped feedback of drunken behavior, and blood alcohol discrimination training. Whether moderation or abstinence were attainable treatment goals and, if so, for whom, were seen simply as questions to be answered (Vogler, 1972). That questioning approach soon resulted in confrontations with the traditional alcohol community. Many workers in the field did not like our reconsideration of basic assumptions such as abstinence as the only cure for alcoholics. But we were even skeptical of the belief that "alcoholics" are essentially alike and that "alcoholism" is a unitary, progressive "disease." What is "loss of control"? Is "One drink, then drunk" really true? We didn't know for sure. Then came a key question: Could some alcohol abusers learn to drink moderately? That led us into studying different kinds of abusers and discovering that *many abusers can learn moderation*, including a few serious alcohol abusers. However, most serious abusers cannot learn moderation, a fact we have tried to make eminently clear in this book. Many of our serious abusers didn't even feel any-

187

thing at a BA of 55 and even higher. How could such individuals possibly learn to stop at 55 if they drank to get high, which they said was their primary goal? These observations eventually led us into studying tolerance which will be discussed below.

In addition to our experimental research, intensive treatment of problem drinkers in private practice has shaped our understanding of drinking habits and how they affect the daily lives of drinkers and their families. This clinical work has served as the real-life testing ground for creatively combining the strategies we found work best to modify drinking habits.

Through our clinical practice and research, and the research of other investigators, we have found some partial answers to basic questions about alcohol abuse. They are not absolute answers because as new information becomes available, our understanding is modified. Yet today it is possible to draw some general conclusions and make helpful suggestions about drinking, which is just what we've done in this book. In the rest of this section we will review some of these conclusions and provide basic research references for the interested reader.

BIOLOGICAL INFLUENCE

Evidence is scant that biological factors cause alcohol abuse for more than perhaps a small percentage at most of the diverse group we call alcohol abusers. To consider excessive drinking a disease without demonstrating evidence of any physical basis for most abusers is therefore unwarranted, misleading, and we think harmful for reasons detailed in Chapter 1. Perhaps someday we will have good scientific evidence that *some* of the people regarded as serious abusers have a strong biological factor contributing to their drinking problem. But right now we don't have such evidence. Most unsuccessful drinkers are not serious abusers anyway, and they are the ones for whom this book was mainly written.

A common myth proposes that alcoholics experience loss of control of their drinking, often referred to as the "one drink, then drunk" hypothesis. Refuting the loss-of-control hypothesis are studies showing that when sober hospitalized alcoholics were given alcohol in a disguised form (*i.e.,* when they did not know they were drinking alcohol), craving for alcohol and continued consumption did not occur (e.g., Engle & Williams, 1972; Marlatt, Demming, & Reid, 1973; and Merry, 1966). Moreover, other studies (*e.g.,*

Bigelow, Liebson, & Griffiths, 1974; Cohen, Liebson, Faillace, & Allen, 1971) have shown chronic alcoholics who had begun drinking, to limit their consumption when meaningful consequences for doing so were available (such as monetary and social rewards), and even when no consequences were present (*e.g.*, Gottheil, Corbett, Grasberger, & Cornelison, 1971; Paredes, Hood, Seymour, & Gollob, 1973). From these studies we conclude that the drinking of known alcoholics is subject to their voluntary and in many cases precise control, given appropriate circumstances.

SOCIAL FACTORS

In general, varying rates of alcohol abuse between different cultures are better explained by the learning conditions and expectations for drinking within a culture than by biological factors. First, the biological evidence is lacking. Second, we find that those cultures which encourage overdrinking (e.g., many northern European countries) as compared to cultures which discourage the excessive use of alcohol (e.g., rural Mediterranean countries), have predictable corresponding differences in alcohol abuse rates.

We know that modeling, or watching and imitating the behavior of others such as parents and peers, is a powerful influence on how people behave (e.g., Bartz & Rasor, 1978). This is true for drinking as well as for other behavior. For example, Caudill & Marlatt (1975) had college students participate in a wine-tasting task with an experimental accomplice who either modeled heavy, light or no consumption. Those subjects exposed to the heavy-drinking accomplice drank more alcohol than did the students exposed to the low or no alcohol consuming models. Similarly, Tomaszewski, Strickler, & Maxwell (1980) found that male college students drank more beer in the company of a beer-drinking companion than with a nondrinking partner or when drinking alone. A survey of 50 hospitalized adolescents who admitted substantial use of alcohol was conducted to determine how the adolescents acquired their drinking habits. The findings strongly implicated a variety of social learning and conditioning factors as responsible for the adolescents' drinking behavior (Stumphauzer, 1980). During a wine-tasting task, alcoholics were exposed to either a heavy- or light-drinking experimental accomplice posing as an alcoholic (Caudill & Lipscomb, 1980). The results once again showed that even the alcoholics varied their drinking according to that of the experimental accomplice. Besides showing the influence of modeling on drinking, this study is also an example of research that fails to support the loss-of-control hypothesis. These and many other studies like them have clearly shown that the drinking behavior of normal drinkers and even alcoholics can be modified by social learning factors.

A more in-depth account of social learning factors and related issues is found in Weissbach & Vogler (1977), Vogler, Compton, & Weissbach (1976), and for German-speaking readers, Vogler & Revenstorf (1977), which is also available in Spanish (1978).

MODERATION

Moderation is possible for many abusers. In two of our major research projects, chronic alcoholics (serious abusers) and problem drinkers (mainly mild and moderate abusers) were trained for moderation using different combinations of techniques (Vogler, Compton, & Weissbach, 1975; Vogler, Compton, Weissbach, & Martin, 1977; Vogler, Weissbach, & Compton, 1977). Two-thirds of the problem drinkers and one-third of the chronic alcoholics drank moderately over the 18-month follow-up period. We conclude, then, that even some chronic serious abusers can learn to drink moderately. And moderation was achieved for a *majority* of the problem drinkers. Our research is only a part of the growing body of evidence demonstrating controlled drinking by alcohol abusers, including some diagnosed as alcoholics (*e.g.*, Hunt & Azrin, 1973; Pomerleau, Pertschuk, Adkins, & Brady, 1978; Popham & Schmidt, 1976; Silverstein, Nathan, & Taylor, 1974).

Thus, there is substantial evidence that directly contradicts the traditional belief that once an abuser, always an abuser. Yet very few practitioners or lay people are aware of this scientific evidence.

Our data show that the chance of success in moderation is related to lower pretreatment alcohol intake, fewer years of abusive drinking, and fewer job, health, and legal problems as a result of drinking—information we have used in our Drinking Survey in Chapter 6. Our subsequent research on tolerance (Banks, Vogler, & Weissbach, 1979; Benton, Banks, & Vogler, 1982; Vogler, 1982; Vogler, Banks, & Benton, submitted) adds sensitivity to lower BA levels as another important factor in evaluating abusiveness and predicting success in moderation—information that is also included in the Drinking Survey. Perhaps more importantly, our tolerance research has shown us that people enjoy drinking the most when their BA is rising, not when it is falling, and that positive subjective benefits from drinking diminish after about an hour of drinking and above a BA of 55 for most drinkers.

THE 55 LIMIT

While there is nothing absolute about a BA of 55 as the upper limit for successful drinking, there are many good reasons for it. Our tolerance research referenced above, and its application in our clinical practice, serve as the primary basis for regarding 55 as the limit to the subjectively experienced benefits from drinking for most successful drinkers. Of course tolerance from prior drinking makes 55 too low for some heavy drinkers to experience the subjective changes they seek from drinking. For them the negative effects on health may be the more important reason for limiting their BA to 55 (the health risks of heavy drinking are well described in "Biomedical Consequences of Alcohol Use and Abuse," in the *Fourth Special Report to the U.S. Congress on Alcohol and Health*, 1981). Acceleration of physical impairment and driving ability with BAs over 55 is well documented in the research literature (e.g., see the review by Levine, 1972; and see Clayton, 1980; Moskowitz, 1971). The finding that alcohol relieves tension up to 55 and then increases it above that level is reported by Allman, Taylor, & Nathan (1972), Marlatt (1976), and Steffan, Nathan, & Taylor (1974).

THE PROBLEM WITH SCIENTIFIC EVIDENCE

The reason most people don't know or accept what we are saying here is that they are not aware of or do not value scientific evidence. The majority of alcohol counselors are "recovering alcoholics," sincere in their desire to help but untrained in the methods of science. They, and even other workers with clinical but not scientific training, have little appreciation for information obtained through experimental study (which is really only a tool for eliminating bias to obtain objectivity in answering questions). Their conclusions are based on personal experiences with alcohol or their acceptance of a cut-and-dried philosophy such as that of Alcoholics Anonymous. They simply lack the breadth of training to understand or appreciate the significance of objective evidence. Certainly we believe that personal and clinical experiences are an important source of ideas, but ideas about human behavior must be evaluated by the objective methods of science before we can accept them as valid. Nevertheless, it is people with untested opinions who dominate the alcohol field and, sadly enough, they respect little else but their own point of view. It is their ideas that the public has heard for decades rather than the new and emerging ones we have presented in this book.

We note, however, that even traditional workers who believe in the disease approach actually *use* some form of learning or experience to help abusers change. Alcoholics Anonymous stresses good modeling for enjoyment of the sober life, reinforcement (praise and encouragement) for being sober, cognitive restructuring of the desire to use alcohol, motivational procedures via group influence, and so on. There is a significant absence of anything physical or "medicinal," as you might expect for a disease. Alcohol education and traditional alcohol counseling rely heavily on learning experiences, specifically on a verbal analysis of drinking and a change in living experiences, to "cure the disease of alcoholism." Raleigh Hills and Schick–Schadel hospitals use aversion conditioning, a straightforward learning technique, as the central component of their treatment programs. We, too, have used aversion in some of our early research, and have concluded that aversion conditioning has limited utility in changing drinking habits permanently (see Vogler, Lunde, Johnson, & Martin, 1970; Vogler, Lunde, & Martin, 1971; Lunde & Vogler, 1970; Vogler, Kraemer, Ferstl, & Brengelmann, 1971; Vogler, Ferstl, Kraemer, & Brengelmann, 1975). So when it comes right down to doing something about the misuse of alcohol, most workers, regardless of orientation, actually *use* some form of learning, albeit unsystematically and often unwittingly. In contrast, this book explicitly uses scientific information and learning principles in a systematic way to teach people how to become and remain successful drinkers.

In summary, the important benefits of the learning approach are:

1. We can identify *degrees* of the learned habit and greatly help those with a mild to moderate habit before it becomes more difficult to change.
2. We can use the demonstrated power of clinically proven learning principles and techniques.
3. We can *prevent* drinking problems altogether by fostering conditions that encourage nondrinking or successful drinking through good modeling, access to practical and meaningful

information, guidelines for successful drinking, and incentives to drink right.

Society has been limited long enough by traditional unquestioned thinking about alcohol and methods of treatment for alcohol abuse. It is time that something better be offered to people who are concerned about drinking. We expect our approach ultimately to improve the quality of life for millions of people whose lives are affected by alcohol.

References

Allman, L. R., Taylor, H. A., and Nathan, P. E. "Group drinking during stress: Effects on drinking behavior, affect, and psychopathology." *American Journal of Psychiatry* 29 (1972):669–78.

Banks, W. P., Vogler, R. E., and Weissbach, T. A. "Adaptation of ethanol intoxication." *Bulletin of the Psychonomic Society* 14 (1979):319–22.

Bartz, W. R., and Rasor, R. A. *Surviving With Kids.* San Luis Obispo, CA.: Impact Publishers, 1978; New York: Ballantine Books, 1980.

Benton, R. P., Banks, W. P., and Vogler, R. E. "Carryover of tolerance to alcohol in moderate drinkers." *Journal of Studies on Alcohol,* 1982.

Bigelow, G., Liebson, I., and Griffiths, R. R. "Alcoholic drinking: Suppression by a behavioral time-out procedure." *Behavior Research and Therapy,* 12 (1974), 107–15.

Carroll, R. B. "Gas-liquid chromatography of whiskies by direct injection." *Journal of Studies on Alcohol* (1972), Supplement 5.

Caudill, B. D., and Lipscomb, T. R. "Modeling influences on alcoholics' rates of alcohol consumption." *Journal of Applied Behavior Analysis* 13 (1980):355–65.

Caudill, B. D., and Marlatt, G. A. "Modeling influences in social drinking: An experimental analogue." *Journal of Consulting and Clinical Psychology* 43, (1975), 405–15.

Clayton, A. B. "Effects of alcohol on driving skills." In M. Sandler (Ed.), *Psychopharmacology of Alcohol.* New York: Raven Press, 1980.

Cohen, M., Liebson, I. A., Faillace, L. A., and Allen, R. P. "Moderate drinking by chronic alcoholics." *Journal of Nervous and Mental Disease* 153 (1971), 434–44.

Engle, K. B., and Williams, T. K. "Effect of an ounce of vodka on alcoholics' desire for alcohol." *Quarterly Journal of Studies on Alcohol* 33 (1972), 1099–1105.

Fourth Special Report to the U.S. Congress on Alcohol and Health from the Secretary of Health and Human Services (DHHS Publication No. ADM 81–1080). Washington D.C.: U.S. Government Printing Office, 1981.

Gottheil, E., Corbett, L. O., Grasberger, J. C., and Cornelison, F. S. "Treating the alcoholic in the presence of alcohol." *American Journal of Psychiatry* 128 (1971), 107–12.

194

Honismann, J. J. "Alcohol in its cultural context." In M. Marshall (Ed.), *Beliefs, Behaviors, Alcoholic Beverages.* Ann Arbor: University of Michigan Press, 1979.

Hunt, G. M., and Azrin, N. H. "The community-reinforcement approach to alcoholism." *Behavior Research and Therapy* 11 (1973), 91–104.

Kozararevic, Dj., et al. "Frequency of alcohol consumption and morbidity and mortality: The Yugoslavia Cardiovascular Disease Study." *The Lancet,* 1 (1980):613–16.

Levine, J. M., Kramer, G. G., and Levine, E. N. "Effect of alcohol on human performance: An integration of research findings based on an abilities classification." *Journal of Applied Psychology* 60 (1972):285–93.

Lunde, S. L., and Vogler, R. E. "Generalization of results in electrical aversion conditioning studies." *Behavior Research and Therapy* 8 (1970):313–14.

Marlatt, G. A. "Alcohol, stress, and cognitive control." In C. D. Spielberger and I. G. Sarabon (Eds.), *Stress and Anxiety,* Vol. 3. Washington D.C.: Hemisphere Publishing Co., 1976.

Marlatt, G. A., Demming, B., and Reid, J. B. "Loss of control drinking in alcoholics: An experimental analogue." *Journal of Abnormal Psychology* 81 (1973), 233–41.

Merry, J. The "loss of control" myth. *Lancet* 1 (1966), 1267–68.

Paredes, A., Hood, W. R., Seymour, H., and Gollob, M. "Loss of control in alcoholism: An investigation of the hypothesis, with experimental findings." *Quarterly Journal of Studies on Alcohol* 34 (1973), 1146–61.

Pomerleau, O. F., Perschuk, M., Adkins, D., and Brady, J. P. "A comparison of behavioral and traditional treatment for middle income problem drinkers." *Journal of Behavioral Medicine* 1 (1978), 187–200.

Popham, R. E. and Schmidt, W. "Some factors affecting the likelihood of moderate drinking by treated alcoholics." *Journal of Studies on Alcohol* 37 (1976), 868–82.

Moskowitz, H. "The effects of alcohol on performance in the driving simulator of alcoholics and social drinkers." Report ENG–7205, Institute of Transportation and Traffic Engineering, U.C.L.A., 1971.

Second Special Report to the U.S. Congress on Alcohol and Health: New Knowledge from the Secretary of Health, Education, and Welfare (DHEW Publication No. ADM 75–212). Washington, D.C.: U.S. Government Printing Office, 1974.

Silverstein, S. J., Nathan, P. E., and Taylor, H. A. "Blood alcohol level estimation and controlled drinking by chronic alcoholics." *Behavior Therapy* 5 (1974), 1–14.

Steffan, J. J., Nathan, P. E., and Taylor, H. A. "Tension-reducing effects of alcohol: Further evidence and some methodological considerations." *Journal of Abnormal Psychology* 83 (1974):542–47.

Stumphauzer, J. S. "Learning to drink: Adolescents and alcohol." *Addictive Behaviors* 5 (1980):277–83.

Tomaszewski, R. J., Strickler, D. P., and Maxwell, W. A. "Influence of social setting and social drinking stimuli on drinking behavior." *Addictive Behaviors* 5 (1980):235–40.

Vogler, R. E. Symposium chairman, Moderation as an approach in alcohol problems. *Proceedings of the Eighty-First Annual Convention of the American Psychological Association*, 1972, 922.

Vogler, R. E., Lunde, S. E., Johnson, G. R., and Martin, P. L. "Electrical aversion conditioning with chronic alcoholics." *Journal of Consulting and Clinical Psychology* 34 (1970):302–7.

Vogler, R. E., Kraemer, S., Ferstl, R., and Brengelmann, J. C. "Aversion conditioning with severe alcoholics." In the *Proceedings of the Third Annual Congress of the European Behavior Therapy Association*, 1971, 227–32.

Vogler, R. E., Lunde, S. E., and Martin, P. L. "Electrical aversion conditioning with chronic alcoholics: Follow-up and suggestions for research." *Journal of Consulting and Clinical Psychology* 36 (1971):450.

Vogler, R. E., Ferstl, R., Kraemer, S., and Brengelmann, J. C. "Aversion conditioning with German alcoholics: One year follow-up." *Behavior Therapy and Experimental Psychiatry* 6 (1975):171–73.

Vogler, R. E., Compton, J. V., and Weissbach, T. A. "Integrated behavior change techniques for alcoholics." *Journal of Consulting and Clinical Psychology* 43 (1975):233–43.

Vogler, R. E., Compton, J. V., and Weissbach, T. A. "The referral problem in the field of alcohol abuse." *Journal of Community Psychology* 4 (1976):357–61.

Vogler, R. E., Compton, J. V., Weissbach, T. A., and Martin, G. T. "Integrated behavior change techniques for problem drinkers in the community." *Journal of Consulting and Clinical Psychology* 45 (1977):267–79.

Vogler, R. E., and Revenstorf, D. *Alkoholmissbrauch: Sozial-psychologische und lerntheoretische Ansätze (Alcohol Abuse: social-psychological and learning theory approaches)*. München: Urban & Schwarzenberg, 1977. Spanish translation, 1978.

Vogler, R. E., Weissbach, T. A., and Compton, J. V. "Learning techniques for alcohol abuse." *Behavior Research and Therapy* 15 (1977):31–38.

Vogler, R. E. "Successful moderation in a chronic alcohol abuser: the case of Bob S." In P. E. Nathan and W. M. Hay (Eds.), *Clinical Case Studies in the Behavioral Treatment of Alcoholism*. New York: Plenum Publishing Co., 1982.

Vogler, R. E., Banks, W. P., and Benton, R. P. "Tolerance to alcohol in moderate and abusive drinkers." Submitted.

Weissbach, T. A., and Vogler, R. E. "Implications of a social learning approach to the prevention and treatment of alcohol abuse." *Contemporary Drug Problems* 6 (1977):553–68. Special Issue on Public Policy.

Tables

Weight, Drinks, and Blood Alcohol

Successful Drinking Is Under 55

One drink = $\frac{12 \text{ oz.}}{\text{beer}}$ = $\frac{4 \text{ oz.}}{\text{wine}}$ = $\frac{2\frac{1}{2} \text{ oz.}}{\text{fortified wine}}$ = $\frac{1\frac{1}{4} \text{ oz.}}{\text{liquor}}$

90-pound person

Hours since start of drinking	Number of Drinks									
	1	2	3	4	5	6	7	8	9	10
1	25	65	105	145	185	225	270	305	345	385
2	10	50	90	130	170	210	255	290	330	370
3	0	35	75	115	155	195	240	275	315	365
4	0	20	60	100	140	180	215	260	300	340
5	0	5	45	85	125	165	200	245	285	325

100-pound person

Hours since start of drinking	Number of Drinks									
	1	2	3	4	5	6	7	8	9	10
1	20	55	95	130	165	200	245	275	310	345
2	5	40	80	115	150	185	230	260	295	330
3	0	25	65	100	135	170	215	245	280	315
4	0	10	50	85	120	155	200	230	265	300
5	0	0	35	70	105	140	185	215	250	285

110-pound person

Hours since start of drinking	Number of Drinks									
	1	2	3	4	5	6	7	8	9	10
1	15	50	85	115	150	180	215	245	280	315
2	0	35	70	100	135	165	200	230	265	300
3	0	20	55	85	120	150	185	215	250	285
4	0	5	40	70	105	135	170	200	235	270
5	0	0	25	55	90	120	155	185	220	255

120-pound person

Hours since	Number of Drinks									
start of drinking	1	2	3	4	5	6	7	8	9	10
1	15	45	75	105	135	165	195	225	255	285
2	0	30	60	90	120	150	180	210	240	270
3	0	15	45	75	105	135	165	195	225	255
4	0	0	30	60	90	120	150	180	210	240
5	0	0	15	45	75	105	135	165	195	225

130-pound person

Hours since	Number of Drinks									
start of drinking	1	2	3	4	5	6	7	8	9	10
1	15	40	70	95	125	150	180	205	235	260
2	0	25	55	80	110	135	165	190	220	245
3	0	10	40	65	95	120	150	175	205	230
4	0	0	25	50	80	105	135	160	190	215
5	0	0	10	35	65	90	120	145	175	200

140-pound person

Hours since	Number of Drinks									
start of drinking	1	2	3	4	5	6	7	8	9	10
1	10	35	60	85	115	140	165	190	215	240
2	0	20	45	70	100	125	150	175	200	225
3	0	5	30	55	85	110	135	160	185	210
4	0	0	15	40	70	95	120	145	170	195
5	0	0	0	25	55	80	105	130	155	180

150-pound person

Hours since start of drinking	Number of Drinks									
	1	2	3	4	5	6	7	8	9	10
1	10	35	55	80	105	130	155	175	200	225
2	0	20	40	65	90	115	140	160	185	210
3	0	5	25	50	75	100	125	145	170	195
4	0	0	10	35	60	85	110	130	155	180
5	0	0	0	20	45	70	95	115	140	165

160-pound person

Hours since start of drinking	Number of Drinks									
	1	2	3	4	5	6	7	8	9	10
1	5	30	50	75	95	120	145	165	190	210
2	0	15	35	60	80	105	130	150	175	195
3	0	0	20	45	65	90	115	135	160	180
4	0	0	5	30	50	75	100	120	145	165
5	0	0	0	15	35	60	85	105	130	150

170-pound person

Hours since start of drinking	Number of Drinks									
	1	2	3	4	5	6	7	8	9	10
1	5	25	50	70	90	110	135	155	175	195
2	0	10	35	55	75	95	120	140	160	180
3	0	0	20	40	60	80	105	125	145	165
4	0	0	5	25	45	65	90	110	130	150
5	0	0	0	10	30	50	75	95	115	135

180-pound person

Hours since start of drinking	Number of Drinks									
	1	2	3	4	5	6	7	8	9	10
1	0	25	45	65	85	105	125	145	165	185
2	0	10	30	50	70	90	110	130	150	170
3	0	0	15	35	55	75	95	115	135	155
4	0	0	0	20	40	60	80	100	120	140
5	0	0	0	5	25	45	65	85	105	125

190-pound person

Hours since start of drinking	Number of Drinks									
	1	2	3	4	5	6	7	8	9	10
1	0	25	40	60	80	100	120	135	155	175
2	0	10	25	45	65	85	105	120	140	160
3	0	0	10	30	50	70	90	105	125	145
4	0	0	0	15	35	55	75	90	110	130
5	0	0	0	0	20	40	60	75	95	115

200-pound person

Hours since start of drinking	Number of Drinks									
	1	2	3	4	5	6	7	8	9	10
1	0	20	40	55	75	95	110	130	145	165
2	0	5	25	40	60	80	95	115	130	150
3	0	0	10	25	45	65	80	100	115	135
4	0	0	0	10	30	50	65	85	100	120
5	0	0	0	0	15	35	50	70	85	105

210-pound person

Hours since start of drinking	Number of Drinks									
	1	2	3	4	5	6	7	8	9	10
1	0	20	35	55	70	90	105	120	140	155
2	0	5	20	40	55	75	90	105	125	140
3	0	0	5	25	40	60	75	90	110	125
4	0	0	0	10	25	45	60	75	95	110
5	0	0	0	0	10	30	45	60	80	95

220-pound person

Hours since start of drinking	Number of Drinks									
	1	2	3	4	5	6	7	8	9	10
1	0	20	35	50	65	85	100	115	130	150
2	0	5	20	35	50	70	85	100	115	135
3	0	0	5	20	35	55	70	85	100	120
4	0	0	0	5	20	40	55	70	85	105
5	0	0	0	0	5	25	40	55	70	90

230-pound person

Hours since start of drinking	Number of Drinks									
	1	2	3	4	5	6	7	8	9	10
1	0	15	30	50	65	80	95	110	125	140
2	0	0	15	35	50	65	80	95	110	125
3	0	0	0	20	35	50	65	80	95	110
4	0	0	0	5	20	35	50	65	80	95
5	0	0	0	0	5	20	35	50	65	80

240-pound person

Hours since start of drinking	Number of Drinks									
	1	2	3	4	5	6	7	8	9	10
1	0	15	30	45	60	75	90	105	120	135
2	0	0	15	30	45	60	75	90	105	120
3	0	0	0	15	30	45	60	75	90	105
4	0	0	0	0	15	30	45	60	75	90
5	0	0	0	0	0	15	30	45	60	75

250-pound person

Hours since start of drinking	Number of Drinks									
	1	2	3	4	5	6	7	8	9	10
1	0	15	30	40	55	70	85	100	115	130
2	0	0	15	25	40	55	70	85	100	115
3	0	0	0	10	25	40	55	70	85	100
4	0	0	0	0	10	25	40	55	70	85
5	0	0	0	0	0	10	25	40	55	70

260-pound person

Hours since start of drinking	Number of Drinks									
	1	2	3	4	5	6	7	8	9	10
1	0	15	25	40	55	70	80	95	110	125
2	0	0	10	25	40	55	65	80	95	110
3	0	0	0	10	25	40	50	65	80	95
4	0	0	0	0	10	25	35	50	65	80
5	0	0	0	0	0	10	20	35	50	65

DRINK CONVERSION TABLE

Conversion of Wine to "Drinks"		Conversion of 80-Proof Liquor to "Drinks"	
Ounces of Wine	Number of Drinks*	Ounces of 80-Proof Liquor	Number of Drinks†
2	½	1	1
4	1	2	1½
6	1½	3	2½
8	2	4	3
10	2½	5	4
12	3	6	5
14	3½	7	5½
16	4	8	6½
18	4½	9	7
20	5	10	8
22	5½	11	9
24	6	12	9½
26	6½	13	10½
28	7	14	11
30	7½	15	12
32	8		
34	8½		
36	9		
38	9½		
40	10		

*4 ounces of wine (12% table wine) = 1 drink.
†1¼ ounces of 80-proof liquor = 1 drink.

Index